SCHOOL-BASED COLLABORATION WITH FAMILIES

J. Brien O'Callaghan

SCHOOL-BASED COLLABORATION WITH FAMILIES

*Constructing
Family-School-Agency
Partnerships That Work*

Jossey-Bass Publishers · San Francisco

LC225.3
O23
1993

Substantial discounts on bulk quantities of Jossey-Bass books
are available to corporations, professional associations, and other
organizations. For details and discount information, contact the
special sales department at Jossey-Bass Inc., Publishers.
(415) 433-1740; Fax (415) 433-0499.

For sales outside the United States, contact Maxwell Macmillan
International Publishing Group, 866 Third Avenue, New York,
New York 10022.

Manufactured in the United States of America

The paper used in this book is acid-free and meets the
State of California requirements for recycled paper
(50 percent recycled waste, including 10 percent
postconsumer waste), which are the strictest guidelines
for recycled paper currently in use in the United States.

10% POST
CONSUMER
W A S T E

The ink in this book is either soy- or vegetable-based and during the
printing process emits fewer than half the volatile organic compounds
(VOCs) emitted by petroleum-based ink.

Library of Congress Cataloging-in-Publication Data

O'Callaghan, James Brien, date.
    School-based collaboration with families : constructing family–
school–agency partnerships that work / J. Brien O'Callaghan.
       p.   cm.—(The Jossey-Bass social and behavioral science
series and The Jossey-Bass education series)
    Includes bibliographical references (p.   ) and index.
    ISBN 1-55542-527-5
    1. Home and school—United States   2. School psychology—United
States.   3. Problem children—Services for—United States.
I. Title.   II. Series: Jossey-Bass social and behavioral science
series.   III. Series: Jossey-Bass education series.
LC225.3.O23   1993
370.19'31'0973—dc20   93-6573
                                                                 CIP

FIRST EDITION
HB Printing   10 9 8 7 6 5 4 3 2 1   *Code 9328*

A joint publication in

THE JOSSEY-BASS
SOCIAL AND BEHAVIORAL SCIENCE SERIES
and
THE JOSSEY-BASS EDUCATION SERIES

Contents

Preface

As stories of childhood tragedy and failure in the United States have become more and more common in recent years, attention has increasingly turned to the notion of collaboration among families, schools, and community agencies—the major systems responsible for raising children. Over the past two decades or so, hundreds of articles, several books, and scores of public and private program proposals have outlined new approaches to preventing and solving children's problems through systems collaboration. The problem today is not a lack of awareness of the crisis in child rearing and education, but the difficult task of sorting through myriad suggested solutions to find a clear, successful, comprehensive, and cost-effective plan that will work. *School-Based Collaboration with Families* is an attempt to outline such a plan of action.

In the spring of 1983, I began doing family interventions in schools, with school personnel present in the room. This practice grew out of in-service training in family systems theory that I provided to school staff, and it was greatly influenced by my early

experiences as a teacher and guidance counselor at the senior high
school level. From the beginning, the family interventions in the
schools were designed to serve two complementary functions: to
prevent and remediate children's problems and to train staff
members in ecosystems concepts and practices. Children's problems
could be of any variety—educational, behavioral, or psychological—and children of all ages were eligible for referral. Originally
called *family-school consultation,* the name gradually changed to
family-school collaboration, and other more recent terms for it include *school-based collaboration with families, school-based ecosystems collaboration,* and *FACETS*™ (Families and Agencies
Collaborating in Ecosystemic Teams in Schools). Since 1983, several school systems in Connecticut have experimented with the
FACETS collaboration model. Two are using it extensively. To
date, I have conducted over three hundred collaborative team interventions (CTIs) of one to three sessions' duration in schools.

   School-Based Collaboration with Families was written in an
attempt to provide a clear and practical map that will help to take
us from our current state of family and educational crisis to a place
in which we know what to do for children—and we actually do it.
The book describes an ecosystemic collaborative model of assessment and intervention that is school-based and that stresses adult
responsibility for children's success and happiness and low toler-
ance for their failure and unhappiness. The collaborative model
advocates direct, open, and assertive communication between
parents and teachers and the active involvement of children in their
own problem solving. Through the presentation of many case examples I demonstrate the effectiveness of focusing on the child's
ecosystem, that is, the pattern of interacting forces and relationships
around the child.

Who Should Read This Book?

I believe that this is truly a book for our time. Professional therapists, child educators, and other service providers—who face every
day the anguish and frustration that result from unsuccessful individual efforts to motivate and help children—will find in it both
hope and practical strategies. The book clearly describes a collaborative philosophy and program that can dramatically enhance the

ability of service providers to turn the lives of problem children around.

Those who work in schools of education, graduate schools, and schools of professional training, as well as parent educators, public and private policy makers, and others responsible for the education and training of adult managers of children will also find *School-Based Collaboration with Families* of use. It will provide this group of trainers with clear and effective models of child intervention to pass on to tomorrow's service providers, policy makers, and parents.

Overview of the Contents

In Part One of the book, key components, operational mechanics, and case studies of the school-based collaboration model are enumerated and explained. Chapter One presents a brief summary of a common type of family-school problem and describes several kinds of therapist reactions. I make an argument for the use of a school-based ecosystemic collaboration model of prevention and problem solving and describe the key components of the model. Chapter Two outlines the operational mechanics of the school-based model and shows how it could be applied to the case presented in Chapter One. Chapter Three lists and describes the interaction of the players in the larger systems surrounding the child and explains the roles of these players in collaborative team interventions. Chapter Four compares and contrasts the use of directness by the ecosystems consultant with more indirect, strategic, and avoidant approaches widely used in traditional interventions.

Part Two outlines a philosophy and method of raising healthy children that is the foundation of successful collaborative adult management of children. Chapter Five provides new concepts, schemas, and classifications to assist collaborative players in understanding the causes and meanings of child behavior. Chapter Six details intervention strategies for working with specific categories of problem behavior in children.

Case studies involving collaborative team interventions (CTIs) are explicated in Part Three, which includes Chapters Seven through Ten. The studies are grouped into categories based on specific common elements. Chapter Seven deals with collaborative team interventions with children diagnosed as having intrapsychic problems, including neurological, psychiatric, and other disorders. CTIs with children whose adult managers disagree about parenting philosophies are covered in Chapter Eight. Chapter Nine outlines CTIs with children who have underinvolved fathers or mothers. Finally, Chapter Ten gives examples of CTIs with children whose caregivers include grandparents, other members of the extended family, or other involved adults.

Part Four presents clear guidelines for establishing and implementing a school-based ecosystems collaboration program. Chapter Eleven describes the obstacles that face proponents of the ecosystemic approach—"collaborationists"—and provides recommendations for establishing collaborative programs in schools. Chapter Twelve discusses the implications of the collaborative model for families, educators, family therapists, the national leaders of the helping profession, and all who are involved in helping children achieve healthy, balanced lives.

Conclusion

At a time in American society when it is obvious that our families, schools, and communities are in crisis, a new model of prevention and problem solving is immediately needed. Instead of resorting to established, lengthy procedures such as psychological testing, academic tutoring, or individual counseling, the school-based collaboration model speeds the problem-solving process by involving family and other adult managers of children in collaborative diagnosis and treatment. Even when this process entails addressing adult dysfunctions and personal issues, the overwhelming majority of parents and adults show initial or eventual receptivity to school-based collaboration. *School-Based Collaboration with Families* provides its readers with clear instructions in the use of a practical model for working together effectively in the best interests of children and the ecosystems in which they live. The case studies and anecdotes herein are offered to encourage therapists, educators, parents, and other adult managers of children to move beyond blame and helplessness and empower themselves to improve the situation now. In these days of drugs, divorce, and depression, school-based ecosystems collaboration offers perhaps the best hope for the solution to many problems that cannot be solved by independent family, school, and community efforts.

Acknowledgments

I would like to express my appreciation to several people who have been especially helpful in making this book a reality. First, I want to thank a select corps of school social workers, psychologists, principals, pupil services directors, superintendents, and other educators who have allowed me to demonstrate and improve my model in their schools and who have persevered against great odds in their confidence in me. In particular, Carmelia Cassano, DeEtta Breitwieser, and the late Gary McMahon were invaluable sources of support since the beginning of this project. Next, I want to thank Becky McGovern and the staff at Jossey-Bass for their encouragement and their helpful editing of my work. I also want to thank my family and friends for enduring years of lectures on the merits of family-school collaboration. Finally, my deepest gratitude goes to Judy Walczak, whose total and unwavering support, common-sense perspective, and technical assistance made a critical difference in the success of my effort.

Bethel, Connecticut   J. BRIEN O'CALLAGHAN
January 1993

To my mother and father,
Mary O'Callaghan and James O'Callaghan,
who raised me to have an opinion,
to get involved, and to not give up;
and to my sons, Brien and Shannon,
my pride and joy.

The Author

J. BRIEN O'CALLAGHAN is a clinical psychologist and marriage and family therapist whose private practice is located in Brookfield, Connecticut. He received his B.A. degree (1965) *summa cum laude* from Marist College in English, his M.S. degree (1969) from St. John's University in counseling, his Ed.M. degree (1973) from Harvard University in psychology, and his Ph.D. degree (1980) from Georgia State University in clinical psychology.

O'Callaghan has published several articles over the years, most recently on the topic of family-school collaboration. He is a member of the American Psychological Association and a clinical member and approved supervisor in the American Association for Marriage and Family Therapy. O'Callaghan served as assistant professor in the School of Education at Southern Connecticut State University from 1984 through 1986 and currently consults with several Connecticut school systems, where he is involved in his principal professional interest—establishing and supervising ecosystems collaborative models in schools.

SCHOOL-BASED COLLABORATION WITH FAMILIES

Part One

KEY COMPONENTS
OF THE
MODEL

1

A BLUEPRINT
FOR
COLLABORATION

A Mother Labeled Incompetent

Sharon Y. was the mother of two children, Robert, twelve, and Charles, ten. Charles, a fifth-grader, was the more difficult to manage, but Robert, a seventh-grader, was very difficult as well. In school, both children were underachievers who disrupted class and argued with their teachers. They also disobeyed their mother and disappeared from the house whenever they could. Sharon was considered "incompetent" by the school system, the police, and social agencies.

Sharon's background was quite chaotic. She had married when she was only seventeen. Her first husband, the boys' father, had become a drug addict and abandoned the family. Her present boyfriend also had a history of social instability but was currently a positive influence in the home. Sharon had been reported to the Department of Child and Youth Services several times for suspicion of child abuse and neglect. The reasons for referral were many, including the excessive school lateness and absence of the children. Social workers had recommended individual therapy for both boys, but Sharon could not afford to pay for therapy and was embarrassed to ask for free therapy. Sharon had also been hospitalized for six months for depression and had been on medication since her hospitalization.

Robert, the older son, had already been referred to a local psychiatric facility for suicidal ideation and threat, and had been referred from there to a residential psychiatric facility, where he was put on medication and kept for three months. This child was later placed in a self-contained classroom—a special class for children with socio-emotional maladjustment—in school. Five years after the first sign of family difficulty had been noticed, Charles, the younger child, was also referred for self-contained placement. It was at this time that the school requested the help of an ecosystems consultant—a family therapist trained to work with all the systems in the "ecology," or environment, of the problem child.

Situations like the one that Sharon, her family, and the school system were involved in are more and more common in the United States. Therapists who are consulted by families or schools for help in such matters might respond in any of a variety of ways. Some therapists would think that the school had handled the situation appropriately and would reassure the school authorities that they were on the right track. These therapists would likely have been trained in Freudian or other psychodynamic methods (Alexander and French, 1946; Freud, 1965). They would think of problems as residing in the individual child and would recommend such continued individual solutions as educational, psychological, neurological, or psychiatric testing; the use of medications; individual counseling; or placement of various family members in an assortment of specialized educational and/or therapeutic environments in and out of school. Therapists of this type might offer to see one of the family members individually in therapy—probably only one, for purposes of confidentiality—or to consult with school staff on the selection of a specialized environment appropriate for the individual child's pathology or deficit.

Another group of therapists presented with the situation described above might view the problem as a relational or interpersonal, rather than an individual, one. These therapists might have been trained in principles of behavior modification (Bandura, 1969; Tharp and Wetzel, 1969; Ullmann and Krasner, 1965) or behavioral parent training (Berkowitz and Graziano, 1972; Cone and Sloop, 1971; O'Dell, 1974, Patterson, 1971; Patterson and Gullion, 1971; Shah, 1969; Tavormina, 1974; Wahler, Winkel, Peterson, and Morrison, 1971). They would believe that for children to change, parents and teachers must control the contingencies or consequences of the children's behavior. Therapists of this type would want to work with the parent or teacher of the child to arrange for a different management style.

A third group of therapists, a group broadly referred to as family systems therapists, would disagree with the school's management of Sharon's situation and would recommend that the family be seen as a group, preferably in a clinic or private office, or perhaps in a private office in a school by a school professional trained in family systems therapy (Amatea and Fabrick, 1981; Conoley, 1987). These therapists would think of individual child and adult problems as interconnected throughout the whole family system, even across generations, through the feedback loops that bind families in covert rules and homeostatic structures (Bateson, 1972; Bowen, 1978; Haley, 1987; Minuchin, 1974). Therapists in this group would believe that the whole is greater than the sum of its parts and that the parts need to be observed and treated for optimal success. Evidence in the literature demonstrates the significant effects of family therapy interventions (Alexander, Barton, Schiavo, Parsons, 1976; Alexander and Parsons, 1973; Fine, 1992; Gurman and Kniskern, 1978; Klein, Alexander, and Parsons, 1977; Santa Barbara and others, 1979; Szapocznik and others, 1986).

A fourth possible therapeutic response to the situation might be to analyze it as an ecosystem problem—that is, in terms of the social systems that affected it, in this case the family, the school, and the relationship between the family and the school. Therapists taking this approach would have been exposed to writings on ecological assessment and intervention (Apter, 1982; Auerswald, 1968; Bronfenbrenner, 1979; Hobbs, 1966, 1975; Hobbs and others, 1984; Minuchin, 1970) and on the functioning of institutions in the larger system, such as schools, hospitals, and courts (Carl and Jurkovic, 1983; Elizur and Minuchin, 1989; Imber-Black, 1988). Therapists of this type would be likely to recommend systems assessment and intervention in more than one environment (home, school, and hospital) or perhaps a collaborative meeting of all the relevant parties in a child's life (for example, parents, teachers, and extended family) at the setting where the problem is presented, in this case the school (Aponte, 1976; Tucker and Dyson, 1976). The meetings at school would be structured interventions, clinic- or private therapist-directed, and would be seen as an adjunct to primarily clinic- or private-based therapy. Some of the collaborative work might be done by telephone, without a therapist visiting the school (Lusterman, 1985, 1992). In this ecosystemic, or "systems-ecological," type of therapy (Fine, 1992), teachers, parents, and relevant others would be clients or consultees of a therapist/consultant who would orchestrate the interactions among them (Aponte, 1976; DiCocco and Lott, 1982; Ron, Rosenberg, Melnick, and Pesses, 1990).

A fifth and final therapeutic response to Sharon and her situation might be influenced by ecosystemic and collaborative thinking. However, therapists holding this viewpoint would consider the primary locus of intervention to be the school and the therapeutic goal to be the training of all school staff in principles of ecosystemic assessment and intervention as well as collaborative team intervention in the family's problems. In this approach, of which there are few examples in the literature to date, the teacher, parents, and other relevant school, family, and community participants are true colleagues and collaborators in an equal partnership, and the ecosystemic consultant works with them within the context of the school's responsibility for problem solving. The school coordinator provides and monitors referrals to outside therapists and agencies. In the literature to date, ecosystemic models of intervention are not primarily school-based, but clinic-based; and school-based models are not primarily ecosystemic, but rather individual and intrapsychic. Neither clinic-based nor school-based interventions are generally collaborative, that is, involving teachers and parents as partners in the process.

Of the many ways that therapists can react to family and

school situations like that presented at the opening of this chapter, in my experience the therapies that look at the largest picture and involve the most people will generally be the most successful. I further believe that therapist activity directed at empowering teachers and parents to assume responsibility for working together in the education and raising of children is the most efficient and effective use of the therapist/consultant's time and expertise.

Families and Schools in a State of Emergency

There are many social and cultural situations in which therapists can take their time debating the efficacy of various therapies and experimenting with one after the other. But in American society today, problems are so pressing that they require an immediate and dramatic shift in the way therapists do business.

Many children are living in family, school, and community structures that are in a state of crisis or simply not working. Children are being abused and neglected in record numbers. *Time* magazine expressed the extent of the problem in terms of the following grim statistics: "Every eight seconds of the school day, a child drops out. Every 26 seconds, a child runs away from home. Every 47 seconds, a child is abused or neglected. Every 67 seconds, a teenager has a baby. Every seven minutes, a child is arrested for a drug offense. Every 36 minutes, a child is killed or injured by a gun. Every day 135,000 children bring guns to school. Even children from the most comfortable surroundings are at risk" (Gibbs, 1990, pp. 42-43).

In the same article, Robert Coles, a noted Harvard psychiatrist, was quoted as saying, "Children who go unheeded . . . are children who are going to turn on the world that neglected them" (p. 43). And Marion Wright Edelman of the Children's Defense Fund added, "The inattention to children by our society poses a greater threat to our safety, harmony, and productivity than any external enemy" (p. 43). The present system of therapy, still primarily individual and, in any case, primarily based at and directed through clinics, is not making a noticeable difference in this situation. The problems are of such enormous proportions that I believe that even a hundred times the present number of private and clinic-based therapists could not get the job done using the current models of intervention.

In the schools the lack of success of individual interventions with difficult students and families is causing great frustration. Despite the use of a large repertoire of individual strategies—including individual assessment and counseling, peer counseling, group counseling, drug curricula, and residential placements—the dropout, illiteracy, suicide, and pregnancy rates continue to be essentially unaffected. Fewer than 50 percent of American children graduate from high school able to read and write. In baseball, batting .500 is superb, but in schools and families, it is a failing grade. It is just not acceptable by any standard to have one out of two youngsters functioning unsuccessfully in school. Family interventions are, of course, much more promising than those that deal only with individual students, but school personnel are reluctant to adopt systemic practices (Carlson and Sincavage, 1987; Foster, 1984).

In the realm of marriage and the family, therapists are also experiencing frustration as families continue to dissolve and malfunction. Office-based family therapy is less and less often an option, especially for highly stressed single parents, step-families, and two-career families who have little time, money, and patience for therapy, no matter how much they may need it.

The help available to schools and therapists from such community agencies as the police, the courts, and public social agencies is often seen as extremely limited and a last resort. Although these systems are theoretically natural partners with schools and therapists, in reality they seldom collaborate and tend to get involved in destructive triangles (Carl and Jurkovic, 1983; Elizur and Minuchin, 1989; Hoffmann and Long, 1969; Miller, 1974). For example, parents who have been reported for child abuse may receive advice and supervision from two or more service providers. A private therapist may recommend a particular method of non-abusive child management, while a worker from the Department of Child and Youth Services may disagree with the therapist's method and send the client "shopping" for a different approach. The lack of collaboration between the providers may be indirect, through failure to communicate with each other, or direct through overt disagreement and conflict. As a result of this triangulation, the client may be confused or may use the opportunity to avoid any therapy or change.

Within community agencies, staff often feel cut off from other systems and unable to do anything of more than short-term benefit, such as refer a child for residential treatment. Finally, families, for their part, are looking for help, but they are unlikely to go to clinics and feel more comfortable in schools (Andolfi, Stein, and Skinner, 1977; Braden and Sherrard, 1987; Conti, 1971, 1973, 1975; Zins and Hopkins, 1981).

All these factors add up to an imperative: private- and clinic-based therapists need to get out of their offices and into schools and join school-based therapists in training all school personnel in ecosystemic thinking and practices, rather than simply focus on case-by-case family intervention. Indeed, for some time school professionals have been recommending the development of effective school-based ecosystemic models (Carlson and Sincavage, 1987; Knox, 1981; Nicoll, 1984).

A School-Based Model

School-based ecosystems collaboration is an educational and therapeutic model whose goal is the prevention or brief remediation of child psychological, academic, and behavioral problems, whether evidenced at home or at school. This model can be utilized with children of all ages, educational levels, and cultural backgrounds, and with any type of child problem. As its title suggests, this particular model consists of school-based, ecosystemic, and collaborative components. The remainder of this chapter focuses on six aspects of these components of the school-based ecosystems collaboration model.

School as Work Site

Probably as long as there have been schools, they have been recognized as partners with parents not only in the education but in the socialization of children. It is apparently only in the past few decades that the partnership between home and school has deteriorated in reaction to teacher demands for higher salaries, increased emphasis on parents' rights, and greater mutual blaming for the increasing academic and behavior problems of children, among other factors (Woody, Yeager, and Woody, 1990). As Scholastic Aptitude Test (SAT) scores have dropped and as more students have dropped out, families have blamed schools. Reciprocally, as students have come to school less prepared, without their homework, and with disrespectful attitudes, educators have blamed divorced, single-parent, remarried, and two-career families. Such community agencies and institutions as police, courts, recreational organizations, and town vendors have begun to blame both the family and school for problems with youth—as families and schools are turning to these community organizations for greater understanding and support.

In this charged and critical atmosphere, it is increasingly clear that the standard, independent, primarily disconnected efforts made by these social systems—family, school, and community—are not working and are not going to work (Okun, 1984; Tucker and Dyson, 1976). But there is disagreement and territorial politicking over what kinds of services are most needed, who should provide these services, and where they should be provided. On any given day, the newspapers, television, and radio propound that the answers to our problems are greater gun control, condom distribution, helicopter raids on Colombian drug barons, more teachers, more police, more prisons, stiffer penalties, and free needles for drug users. My belief is that the best service for children is provided in problem-solving sessions involving all the adult managers of children (principally parents and teachers) and the children themselves, who ultimately are their own best managers. Moreover, I believe that the best site for this effort is the school—for several reasons:

1.   Children are in school at least six hours a day and spend more time there than anywhere else but home. Including before and after school programs, children sometimes spend more awake time in school than at home on school days—which make up at least half the year.

2.   Besides their parents, children's teachers often know them better than anyone. Teachers are frequently deeply concerned about the children in their care. Educators collaborate in interventions for children more than members of any other single group.

Because teachers are invaluable assets in collaborative efforts for children, access to teachers is, by itself, a sufficient defense of the primacy of school-based services. The only practical way to facilitate teachers' involvement in solving child problems is to bring others to school rather than send school professionals elsewhere.

3. Parents, the primary managers of children and the most important players in the interactive, ecosystemic context, generally trust teachers and other educators (for example, principals)—or are at least more open to them and interact with them more than with most other professionals. Some observers have emphasized the barriers between parents and teachers (Foster, 1984; Lightfoot, 1978); however, in my experience, parents still often perceive the school as a safe environment and a place conducive to the honest family discussions that are necessary in most situations in which children have problems.

4. There is a veritable army of helping professionals in school, many of whom are involved at the same time with the same child. Particularly when a family has more than one child in a school or school district, dozens of educators may be involved with that family. An individual family therapist or agency case worker cannot provide the extent of care available from a group of concerned educators trained in ecosystemic thinking and intervention strategies.

Ecosystemic Assessment and Intervention

Ecosystemic assessment and intervention can occur anywhere—at home, at school, or in a clinical or community setting. The intervention can be educational, clinical, nutritional, medical, or of some other type. The term *ecosystemic* is an amalgam of two terms, *systemic* and *ecological,* which refer to two complementary and partially overlapping approaches to assessment and treatment. The systemic approach derives from general systems theory (Bateson, 1972; von Bertalanffy, 1958) and is articulated most clearly by such systems therapists as Bowen (1978), Haley (1987), Minuchin (1974), de Shazer (1982, 1985), and others, who tend to have their own idiosyncratic models of systems therapy (for example, Haley's Problem-solving Therapy). One of the principal concepts of sys-

tems theory is that individual behavior is best understood as interactive communication in relationship to others (for example, parents and teachers), in a social context, as opposed to a nonsocial
effect of intrapsychic processes (for example, drives or impulses).
The ecological approach stems from the work of Apter (1982),
Barker (1965), Bronfenbrenner (1979), Hobbs (1966, 1975), Willems
(1974), Wright (1970), and others, and expands the notion of system
by introducing the more generalized concepts of environment, habitat, and climate. The concept of ecology suggests the interactions
of systems such as home and school in a larger system analysis.
Viewing a child from the ecosystemic perspective requires a consideration of all the forces that may interact in the child's life. A child's
primary environments are the home, school, and community, and
the primary forces affecting a child are the child's own biological
health, the quality of the physical habitat (for example, the air,
water, and food), and the quality of the psychological habitat (for
example, the relationship between the child and his or her parents,
teachers, and siblings). (For excellent discussions of the systems-
ecological perspective and its application to home-school intervention, see Carlson, 1992; Fine, 1992; and Plas, 1992.)

At the time of writing, there are several hundred articles and
a handful of books that focus on the utilization of the systemic or
ecosystemic perspective in solving child home and school problems
(Anderson, 1983; Aponte, 1976; Carlson, 1992; Conoley, 1987; Di-
Cocco, 1986; Dombalis and Erchul, 1987; Fine, 1984, 1992; Fine and
Holt, 1983; Fish and Jain, 1988; Friesen, 1976; Golden, 1983; Goldenberg and Goldenberg, 1981; Goodman and Kjonaas, 1984; Kramer, 1977; Lombard, 1979; Loven, 1978; Perosa and Perosa, 1981;
Plas, 1986; Quirk and others, 1987; Worden, 1981). These studies are
written for various populations, for example, family therapists,
school psychologists, and school counselors, but all consider in
some way the interplay between the home and school environments,
with occasional reference to community subsystems, such as family
court or child welfare agency. The general format in these studies
is a description of family systems theory and the presentation of case
studies in which systems principles are used to solve child problems
in school or in a setting out of school. Some articles deal with
special topics and issues, such as training, confidentiality, and the

similarities and differences between home and school. Although all these efforts are at least systemic, if not ecosystemic, in nature, one or the other system in the overall ecology of home, school, and community tends to be emphasized or treated separately. When a child's parents divorce, for example, a school system may offer a divorce group or individual counseling to the child in school while the parents work independently on their issues out of school (Berger, Shoul, and Warschauer, 1992). In another scenario, the school mental health professional, although he or she may believe in the interactive circular relationship of home and school behavior, will refer the child with a school problem for office-based family therapy to solve the problem that presents itself in school (Amatea and Fabrick, 1984; Nicoll, 1984; Wattenberg and Kagle, 1986). Finally, an office-based therapist working with a family that reports a school problem may choose to discuss the problem over the phone with school personnnel but to not visit the school, meet with school personnel in person, or interview the family and school personnel together (Lusterman, 1985, 1992). The school-based ecosystems collaborative model uses an ecosystemic model of assessment and intervention which, in addition, is based and coordinated in school and involves the collaboration of all the relevant "players" in the child's life.

The School Subsystem

Many writers have discussed the organizational structure and "culture" of the school (Coleman, 1987; Foster, 1984; Lightfoot, 1978), and its level of openness to parents and families (London, Molotsi, and Palmer, 1984). In an analysis of school structure, roles, and rules, many researchers mention such concepts as territoriality, fear, individualism, and other obstacles to ecosystemic collaboration. Writers on school consultation generally recommend strategic, indirect, and sensitive handling of educators, a "gentle leaning" approach (Eno, 1985), which respects the school's boundaries and recognizes a wide variety of educational triangulating within the school (Minard, 1976). In addition, school personnel have probably been trained in an intrapsychic, individual mode of thinking that did not prepare them for a contextual understanding of problems or for relating to parents (Carlson, 1992; Conoley, 1987).

The adoption of the school-based ecosystems collaboration model requires what Thomas Kuhn called a paradigm shift in educator thinking and training (Kuhn, 1970). Although this might seem to be a formidable obstacle, it seems clear that motivation to solve the problems at hand plays a large part in driving such changes. School personnel are themselves members of families, and most have children who attend school. Their interest in addressing the crises in the family and schools is vested in both their personal and in their professional lives. As educators gain knowledge of and experience with the ecosystem approach, there is no doubt of the appeal of the collaborative model. Indeed, many studies indicate an increasing interest in ecosystemic training and recognition of the need for it (Carlson, 1992; Carlson and Sincavage, 1987; Conoley, 1987; Green and Fine, 1980; Knox, 1981; Nicoll, 1984; Pfeiffer and Tittler, 1983; Palmo, Lowry, Weldon, and Scoscia, 1984).

The Family Subsystem

For a child to be "cured" of a home or school problem that is not primarily biological, medical, or financial—and this covers the vast majority of child "problems," including those of inner-city children—family relationships need to change. Boundaries need to become either less diffuse or less rigid (Minuchin, 1974); parents need to exercise either more or less protection or control; adult individual and marital problems need to be resolved. This component of the model is clinical and involves dealing in school with marital and family issues. The notion of using the school as the primary site for family restructuring is probably this book's most controversial feature. By and large, the ecosystemic literature cautions against the use of the school as a clinical setting. Many maneuvers are offered for avoiding discussion of "sensitive" family issues and for referring families to resources outside the school when these matters arise. The use of such tactics to disengage the school continue in spite of wide recognition of the influence of family functioning on school behavior and performance (Barkley, 1981; Carlson and Sincavage, 1987; Dreikurs and Soltz, 1964; Ehrlich, 1983; Fine and Jennings,

1985, 1992; Friedman, 1969; Miller and Westman, 1964; Patterson, DeBarsyske, and Ramsey, 1989; Smith, 1978; Staver, 1953). In addition, the practice of referring school problems outside of school continues in spite of awareness of the difficulty of making successful referrals (Conti, 1971, 1973). In the school-based ecosystems collaboration model, relevant issues, including marital dysfunction and parent disagreements about parenting, are dealt with in collaborative school meetings, if not earlier, in more private teacher-parent interaction. In addition to clincial assessment and intervention, it is important, within this model, to provide parents with an effective parenting philosophy and set of strategies that is consistent with ecosystemic concepts (Fine and Jennings, 1985, 1992).

The Family-School Relationship

In addition to the school and family, there is another subsystem possibly more important than either, namely, the family-school subsystem. Most articles that recognize the importance of the family in school performance make reference to the child's role as a "go-between," connecting the home and school systems and carrying messages back and forth between them. The difficulty of pleasing both systems when they have different values or rules is frequently noted (Aponte, 1976; Carl and Jurkovic, 1983; Green, 1985; Power and Bartholemew, 1985). Several authors have developed categories of family-school relationships, types of triangles, and stages of the family-school relationship (Compher, 1982; DiCocco, 1986; DiCocco and Lott, 1982; Foster, 1984, Power and Bartholemew, 1987).

The three key variables in the family-school discussion are the locus of assessment intervention, who is responsible for the resolution of family-school problems, and how problem resolution is accomplished.

On the first issue, the literature overwhelmingly recommends clinic-based or office-based mental health programs in which schools are involved as information providers, referral sources, or occasional participants in collaborative school sessions, with parents, and sometimes children, present (Taylor, 1982, 1986; Foster, 1984; Aponte, 1976). Other writers do encourage intervening in school (Amatea and Fabrick, 1981; Fine and Holt, 1983; Conoley,

1987). (My own position, which I elaborate elsewhere, is that the primary site of child problem solving should be the school.)

It is a corollary of the first point that the school should take the lead in child problem solving, whether the problems present themselves at home or in school. While problems may be primarily family-based, they usually have a direct effect on school performance. Families often do not know what to do to solve the problem, or they may be unable to solve the problem without help. Again, most of the literature describes clinic-based efforts, resulting from school referral, in which the primary responsible agent is the private or clinic therapist. In addition, in the school-based examples given in the literature, the primary responsible agent is the school mental health or pupil personnel worker (for example, the school psychologist, the school social worker, or the school guidance counselor). In the model presented in this book, the primary agent of responsibility is the classroom teacher, who is supported in his or her work by mental health and other consultants. The rationale for this designation is the amount of contact between teacher and student and, potentially, between teacher and parent. The teacher-parent-child relationship is the fundamental unit of interaction in the school-based ecosystems collaboration model. In contrast, in most of the family intervention and collaborative literature, the teacher, like the parent, is treated as a client of clinic-based or school-based mental health workers.

This leads to the third point of discussion—the method of treatment. As we have seen, the prevailing model of systems problem solving is based on in-school or out-of-school orchestration of change by mental health workers. In this model, mental health practitioners receive referrals from teachers or self-referrals from parents and do family therapy that is disconnected from school and from school teachers. Private therapists sometimes involve school personnel, and occasionally come to school. Some recommend telephone contact as a primary means of family-school collaboration (Lusterman, 1985). School practitioners may or may not involve teachers in interventions with children and their families because such matters are seen as outside their realm of concern. The manner in which school practitioners deal with teachers and parents is described as "strategic," a term that suggests a relationship in which the client, namely, child, parent, or teacher, is manipulated into change by the provider, often without the client's full understanding or cooperation. If families and schools are going to be truly effective at solving child problems, they are going to have to adopt a more collaborative, non-hierarchical approach to this process in which the boundary between provider and client is less rigid and there is an open and honest flow of communication among all concerned.

The Larger System

The success of the collaborative model depends, to some extent, on school assumption of leadership in work with components of the larger system—the police, the courts, social agencies, hospitals, private therapists, and other entities—in the interest of children. The ways in which institutions in the larger system help or hinder ecosystemic efforts for children is addressed by Elizur and Minuchin (1989), Imber-Black (1988), and Jackson (1967), among others. Psychiatric hospitals, for example, can either accept a child as an individual patient in residential treatment or they can refer the entire family of the patient to community-based family therapy or to school-based collaborative intervention. In another situation, a pediatrician can refer a "hyperactive" child to a neurologist or even prescribe Ritalin immediately, or can refer the child for family assessment prior to individually focused intervention. Finally, a private therapist can play chess or basketball for months or years to form a "relationship" with a problem child, or the therapist can learn, or refer the child to, more effective systems therapies. In school-based ecosystems collaboration, the school does not accept a passive or low-profile position in larger system decision-making about child treatment. Because the school is concerned about the total welfare of the child, it takes an active role in determining the value of such treatments as individual hospitalization, medication, and therapy and offers alternative suggestions if warranted.

The Ecosystems Consultant

Although it is possible for a school-based ecosystems collaborative program to be initiated and implemented by a systemically trained school employee with administrative support, the use of an ecosystems consultant or coach, external to the system and with a high degree of expertise in family therapy, in-service training, and organizational consulting is desirable and probably essential. Rhodes (1970) referred to the "consultative orientation" of the helping professional as the "single most important tool in the ecological model." Although the consultative role can be played by the school coordinator, it is often difficult for a full-time employee of the school system to be accepted simultaneously as a colleague or "sibling" and a consultant or trainer. It will be far more productive for the school system to engage an external, independent consultant to assist the participants in communication, boundary setting, cooperation, and keeping the focus on the primary task, which is taking better care of children.

The ecosystemic consultant's role bridges and incorporates many of the traditional approaches, such as client-centered and consultee-centered consultation approaches described in classical texts by Caplan (1970) and Gallessich (1982). The ecosystemic consultant who offers guidance on the interactions and sequences in systems may draw on guidelines provided in newer works on systems consultation (Wynne, McDaniel, and Weber, 1986). It is important to emphasize, however, that the systems consultation called for in the school-based ecosystems collaborative model may combine or transcend program-oriented, agency-oriented or case-based, education-based, and relationship-based functions (Fisher, 1986; Imber-Black, 1988). While some of the ecosystemic consultant's work may fit neatly in one category or another, most of it will take the form of analysis of interactions within and across many systems and the report of this analysis to people who are consultees and clients of consultees. In a collaborative meeting, for example, the consultant's analysis might cover an antagonistic family-school relationship, a conflict between teachers in special education and mainstream classes, a parental disagreement or marital problem at home, and a peer problem at school. This comprehensive analysis might well be provided to all the players in these relationships, meeting together in the same room. The type of consultation described here is relatively unusual and is not used in most schools. It is at once difficult, exciting, and full of potential either for disaster or for dramatic ecosystemic success. As the reader learns more about the school-based ecosystems collaborative model, the value of this role for the family systems therapist will be easier to judge.

Collaboration Among System Players

The dictionary definition for *collaboration* is "the act of working together." The work involved in the ecosystems model is the prevention and solution of child problems. The tools are ecosystemic assessment and intervention techniques. The workers, in addition to the child in each case, are the child's parents, siblings, and extended family, his or her teachers and other educators, and others close to the child, for example, the child's Little League coach. In the school-based model of collaboration, cooperation among players is organized principally at school. It involves ongoing and active monitoring of auxiliary activities and procedures, such as enrollment of a child in summer camp, by the child's teacher or other designated case manager.

The notion of collaboration, general and broad as it is, has become popular in educational systems, where it usually refers to cooperative efforts between mainstream teachers, between mainstream and special education teachers, or among workers in several disciplines in a school, for example, teacher, guidance counselor, school psychologist, and administrator. The practice of family-school collaboration or family-school-community collaboration is not as familiar to educators as is intraschool collaboration, and collaborative school practices involving the family do not usually include in-school discussion of family dynamics. Private therapist collaboration with school personnel and other community providers, similarly, usually involves requests for, or provision of, information for use in individual and separate efforts that may be ecosystemically oriented. The private therapist, for example, may request testing and behavioral information from the school, or answer a request from the Department of Child and Youth Services for verification that the child is attending therapy sessions. McDaniel (1981) was surprised to discover how little contact there was between schools and mental health practitioners and referred to these groups as "disengaged systems."

As we have seen, therapist-school collaboration is usually clinic based (Andolfi, Stein, and Skinner, 1977; Aponte, 1976; Carl and Jurkovic, 1983) and orchestrated by the clinic or private therapist to whom families are referred (Amatea and Fabrick, 1981, 1984; Wattenberg and Kagle, 1986). Indeed, efforts to help children have tended to be of one kind, for example, educational, therapeutic, nutritional, or medical—not all of these—and the collaboration between the providers of these services is usually limited to sharing information, not working closely together across systems. The collaborative nature of the ecosystemic model calls for all the relevant players to meet together at the school when a child's problems are not resolving in response to independent efforts.

Perhaps the most challenging implication of the ecosystemic approach is that all the collaborators are theoretically equal, including the child and the child's siblings. Families and schools are hierarchically organized, so it may be difficult to envision, let alone implement, a true collaboration among parties whose status and power levels are not equal outside the ecosystem context. The reality is that in school-based collaboration, some players, such as parents and administrators, do have more power than others. Further discussion of this model will demonstrate methods by which power can be shared with the officially less powerful—for example, children and teachers—in ways that can enhance their acceptance of responsibility for change and ability to effect it.

Empowerment of the Collaborators

For collaborators to take responsibility for helping children, they need to feel empowered. Dunst and Trivette (1987) have analyzed the research literature on the helping process and have developed a family systems assessment and intervention model based on what they call a "social systems model of functioning." This model was synthesized from a number of conceptual frameworks including human ecology (Bronfenbrenner, 1979), social support theory (Cohen and Syme, 1985), help-seeking theory (DePaulo, Nadler, and Fisher, 1983), adaptational theory (Crnic, Friedrich, and Greenberg, 1983), and self-efficacy theory (Bandura, 1977). Dunst and Trivette

(1987, p. 444) recommend an assessment and intervention model which is based on four substantive principles:

1. Identification of family needs
2. Use of existing family functioning style (strengths and capabilities)
3. Utilization of the family's social network (for example, relatives, neighbors, friends) as a source of support and resources
4. Promotion of the family's acquisition of competencies and skills, that is, empowering the family in self-efficacy

To operationalize empowerment, Dunst and Trivette recommend the adaptation of the following three beliefs (p. 445):

1. People are already competent or able to become competent.
2. Failure to display competence does not result from deficits but from the failure of social systems to create opportunities for competencies to be displayed (enabling experiences).
3. To acquire a sense of control, the learner, client, or recipient of help must attribute behavior change to his or her own actions.

Dunst and Trivette recommend an "enabling" model of helping that leads to family empowerment. According to these authors, the help given in this model (pp. 451–453)

1. Uses care, warmth, and encouragement
2. Uses assertiveness in offering help
3. Leaves the decision to change in the help seeker's hands
4. Offers aid that is normative in the client's culture
5. Provides a solution congruent with the help seeker's way of thinking
6. Offers aid in which the response cost is not greater than the benefits
7. Offers help that can be reciprocated
8. Provides for immediate success in problem solving
9. Promotes the family's use of natural support networks

10. Conveys a sense of cooperation and joint responsibility (partnership) for meeting needs and solving problems
11. Promotes the acquisition of independent and self-sustaining behavior
12. Helps the client to perceive that he or she was the active, responsible, agent of change

The principles identified by Dunst and Trivette (1987) and others on the subject of enablement, empowerment, and self-efficacy (Bandura, 1977; Brickman and others, 1982) form the basis of one of the key components in the present model, that is, the use of a collaborative or partnership approach. The goal of intervention is to transfer the responsibility for change to the front-line players in the ecosystem, the child, his or her family, and his or her teachers. Whereas this goal is, theoretically, present in many helping approaches, the collaborative ecosystemic model offers a means to move quickly and effectively to achieve it. Dunst and Trivette's emphasis on the use of natural resources, family strengths, the acquisition of skills and competencies, and the promotion of a spirit of cooperation, joint responsibility, and partnership are particularly compatible with the goals of the school-based ecosystems collaboration model.

Summary

The case of Sharon Y. is based on a real family and school problem which was treated for five years in an individual, intrapsychic, linear fashion without success. An alternative to those approaches lies in the ecosystemic, school-based, collaborative model, which is based on general systems and ecology theory. In Chapter Two we will return to the case of Sharon Y. and her children and see how the ecosystemic model can be put to use on their behalf.

2

COLLABORATIVE ASSESSMENT AND INTERVENTION

This chapter outlines a step-by-step school-based ecosystemic collaborative assessment and intervention model. The case is that of Sharon Y. and her sons, Robert and Charles, presented in Chapter One. The specifics of this intervention will reveal to readers how the ecosystemic approach works. It is hoped that readers will find their own roles reflected among those of the collaborators in this example.

The Consultant Strategy Meeting

When contacted for help on this case, the ecosystems consultant requested as a first step a meeting of the major players in the school's provider network that were involved in dealing with Sharon Y. and her family. This meeting, called the consultant strategy meeting, was attended by two school social workers, a school psychologist, a guidance counselor, and the director of the pupil

services department of the school district. All of the school personnel at the meeting had been previously exposed to the consultant's
thinking and approach in brief presentations, parenting work-
shops, and in-service training sessions, and were familiar with the
consultant's school-based ecosystems collaboration model. As the
consultant listened to everyone's perspective on the family situation, he drew a diagram on the blackboard showing how the school
and community players interacted with the family and with each
other. The consultant's initial impression was that the family
would be receptive to help, but that they would need strong, philosophically consistent collaborative support. His main concern was
the attitude of one of the teachers of the younger child, Charles, who
apparently conceptualized problems in intrapsychic terms and, in
this case, believed that Charles was learning disabled, suffered from
attention deficit hyperactivity disorder (ADHD), and could not be
educated in a mainstream classroom. The consultant discussed with
the school staff whether they were willing to deal with problems in
the school environment (for example, teacher-student relationship
problems) as well as problems in the home environment and
whether they were willing to deal openly with the parent-teacher
relationship. The school personnel indicated that they were open to
a total systems analysis, but that the consultant should "go easy"
on the school staff initially until school leaders could plan ways of
dealing with school changes that might be recommended. After
hearing the reports and briefly discussing the case, the consultant
recommended a collaborative team intervention (CTI) to be attended by all the relevant players in the home, school, and community ecosystem. This meeting was scheduled for after school on a
school day. The high school was selected as the site because its
meeting room would accommodate the large group of people in a
circular seating arrangement.

The Collaborative Team Intervention

The twenty-two people who attended the first meeting about
Sharon Y. and her sons included members of the immediate family
and the extended family, a local youth officer, and many school
officials involved with Robert and Charles (see Figure 2.1). The

**Figure 2.1. Seating Arrangement for Participants in
the Collaborative Team Intervention Meeting.**

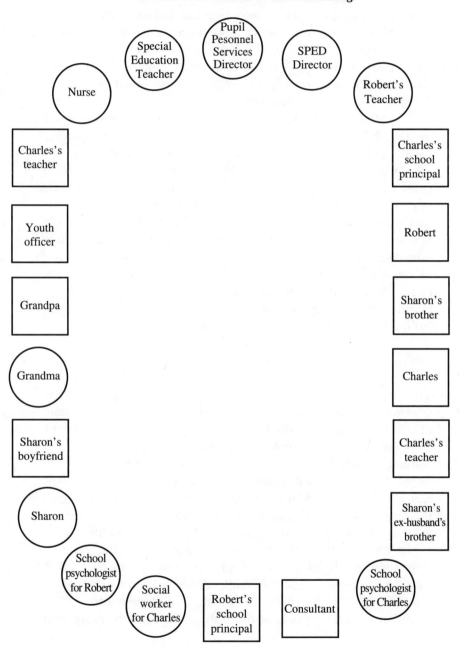

meeting lasted three hours. For the first hour and a half, people gave their accounts and opinions regarding the problem. All twenty-two participants spoke in turn, including the children. During this time, the school coordinator asked questions as necessary to clarify speakers' opinions or points of information. After a short break, the consultant gave his opinion and facilitated a discussion among all those present, focused on the diagnosis and treatment of the children's home and school problems.

The approach taken at the collaborative team intervention meeting combined consultation, therapy, education, and partner collaboration. The consultant's delivery of an expert opinion was acknowledged by all as a part of his job. The discussion included issues that would ordinarily be considered matters for private therapy. With so many participants present, the consultant's comments sometimes took on an educational flavor, like an address to a large audience. However, in an effort to engage participants and minimize distance among them, the consultant made a point of talking to them as friends and colleagues. He also employed many therapeutic skills in his facilitation, including circular questioning, reframing, restraining, provision of examples or anecdotes, establishing "agreements," and use of humor.

Assessment and Intervention

The consultant's diagnosis was that Sharon's children were suffering from what he called motivational deficit disorder (MDD), a state of mind or attitude in which they were unmotivated to achieve or work toward socially acceptable goals like learning to cooperate and empathize with others. Motivational deficit disorder stems from parent training deficit disorder (PTDD) and other disorders in adult management of children in which children are not provided with the proper balance of control and protection necessary for the development of successful and optimistic attitudes toward life.

The consultant recommended more control of the children, positive reframing of the mother's behavior as "uncertain" rather than "incompetent," and reframing of the children's problems as "motivational" rather than "psychiatric" or "educational." The consultant asked for reactions to his diagnosis from the group and for everyone to participate freely in discussing the children's diagnosis and treatment further. Facilitation and direction was now returned to the school coordinator.

As the school coordinator attempted to achieve consensus from the participants at this CTI, significant differences of opinion emerged among the adults. One of Charles's teachers was quite insistent that parent or adult management style was of secondary importance to "learning gaps" and "disabilities" that he thought could only be effectively treated in a special education classroom. Another teacher voiced a dissenting opinion, saying that Charles performed normally in her classroom in response to a nurturing and accepting approach. Sharon was very much in favor of Charles's remaining in mainstream classes. The consultant commented that he thought that learning disabilities were overdiagnosed and that, in any case, attempts to stabilize the family should be given priority over educational changes. He recommended time-out procedures in school or sending Charles home if he became too disruptive. Both Robert and Charles were asked their opinion, but did not offer any comments.

After listening to various suggestions, the principal chose to follow the consultant's suggestions for working with Charles, that is, to leave him in the mainstream classroom. He also recommended that the family find a family therapist to continue the work begun at the CTI. The youth officer suggested that the consultant be designated as the private family therapist, and a school official offered to pay for this work. A follow-up meeting was scheduled for a month later. Extensive communication continued for the remainder of the school year among family, school, community, and consultant.

Results

Seven months of work (the remainder of the school year) with the two children in this family, but more importantly with the adults in their lives, produced stormy, but moderately successful, results. The first private therapy session was three hours in duration and was spent on the floor, with family adults restraining Charles and Robert (their backs flat on the floor) because they were taking turns trying to leave the room and otherwise disrupt the session. Immediate results were achieved in child compliance and cooperativeness as a result of this session, as well as in parent understanding of how to control the children. (Full discussion of the restraining procedure used here will be provided in Chapter Six.)

The school process was much more controversial. As it became more and more clear that, despite student and family improvement, Charles's teacher was not going to change his opinions, the school system's officials had to cope with the situation. After several meetings involving differing combinations of school and family players, and after several discussions with the consultant, the school decided to support the position of the mother, who wanted Charles in the mainstream, and to resist the efforts of his teacher to label him learning disabled and place him in special education. Charles was eventually transferred out of that teacher's class and began to do well in his new mainstream classroom. The mother's relationship with the principal and school psychologist at Charles's school steadily improved.

Although Charles, the primary target of this intervention, was improving, Robert got worse. Robert began talking about not wanting to live anymore and became more disrespectful in his special education classroom, though not in his mainstream classes. The social worker considered him depressed and suicidal, became more convinced of the mother's incompetence, and agitated for another round of medical and psychiatric evaluations of Robert which she hoped would result in the discovery of unresolved trauma from his past and present. She also recommended medication and rehospitalization. Staff members at the school disagreed about Robert's problem, and those responsible for Robert were not sympathetic with ecosystemic ideas and practices. The relationships between Sharon and the principal at Robert's school was not good and was clearly not a collaborative one.

Family therapy with Sharon, her children, Sharon's boyfriend, and occasionally with Sharon's mother, was very positive. Sharon appreciated hearing, for the first time, that she was not incompetent and being supported in her fledgling attempts to gain control of her children. The children profited from discussions of the family's history, principally their father's drug addiction and disappearance. Issues involving Sharon's mother, ex-husband, and particularly, her current boyfriend were dealt with concurrently with child management issues. These tended to fall into a circular pattern in which Sharon would get discouraged and depressed by conflicts with her boyfriend, the misbehavior of her children, or negative innuendo from school staff, and give up the use of her child management techniques. The boys' behavior, in turn, would get worse, leading to further adult conflict and school negativity.

Meetings between Sharon and the consultant in the role of therapist, or between the consultant/therapist and sympathetic school staff, would then interrupt this sequence temporarily, only to have it recur. The therapist obtained additional support for Sharon by referring her to the family officer of the superior court, who provided legal backing for Sharon's authority. The consultant/therapist maintained phone contact with these latter players. As the school year ended, Sharon's mood, enthusiasm, and sense of confidence was significantly higher than they had been seven months earlier. The children were better behaved, but much more change was needed. One of the principals, some of the school staff, and most importantly, the director of pupil services were impressed with Sharon's progress to the extent that they fully accepted the value of school-based ecosystemic collaboration. Other school staff were not impressed and were still attached to their beliefs that the children's problems were the result of intrapsychic disabilities.

Discussion

The assessment of the situation involving Sharon, her children, and their school problems was ecosystemic. It took into account the interactions among many of the players in the children's lives. In addition, the assessment and intervention were school-based. (The family was not referred to a clinic and brought back to the school for one or two sessions within an overall private- or clinic-based family therapy format.) In this case, the school system, through its highest administrative representatives, took responsibility for the solution to this problem and hired a consultant to come to school to train them in ecosystemic thinking and to help them solve the problem. The fact that in this case the consultant was also used as a private therapist for the family is incidental to the principal point—that the school was addressing the problem.

Finally, the assessment and intervention were collaborative. The goal of consultation was the activation of cooperative equal relationships among all parties, including the children, if they chose to participate. The style of the consultation, though initially quite gentle with school staff (Eno, 1985), became progressively more assertive (Andolfi, 1979; Andolfi, Angelo, Menghi, and Nicolo-Corigliano, 1983; Wendt, 1987, 1992) both in school consultations and in joint CTIs. Confidentiality was intentionally disregarded by the consultant because this was a *collaborative* intervention, and he continually reported to all parties what others had said. This open communication approach was upsetting only to school staff committed to an intrapsychic, medical model, not to most of the school staff. The overall result of this model of consultation, which is open and explicit (Paget, 1987), is that more emotionally spontaneous and interactive family-school relationships were established, which is characteristic of healthy family functioning.

Many therapists recommend against dropping communication barriers or boundaries in family-school relationships in cases of high family-school conflict, recommending instead such indirect appoaches as reframing, paradox, and other strategies designed to avoid hostility. The collaboration model is different; open communication, including hostility, is encouraged. In the present case, everyone felt free to speak his or her mind, even though there was much disagreement, and I strongly believe that the open communication was a key to avoiding more restrictive and adversarial outcomes, such as hospitalization, further special education, medication, and a breakdown of cooperation between home and school. (In Chapter Four, the consultant's use of directness that is also positive, supportive, and respectful is discussed in detail.)

By supporting a school-based intervention that was both ecosystemic and collaborative, the school system learned how to better manage one family's children and acquired some fundamental methods for dealing with other difficult families in the future.

The School Decision Chart

In the case of Sharon and her family, the ecosystem of home, school, and community had developed deficits over many years. Dysfunctional interactions, intended as solutions and based on intrapsychic, linear thinking, had only exacerbated the original problem, that is, the ineffective parenting and personal problems of the mother. As with so many child problems, the school was the primary site for presentation of the problems, and members of the school staff were part of the problem. Figure 2.2 presents the interactional steps by which school officials, primarily mainstream teachers, can become involved in organizing solutions to child home, school, and community problems.

The School Decision Chart depicts a progressive flow of school-based interventions in the service of child problem resolution. It calls for the active ownership of responsibility for child success, primarily by the teacher, but also by school administration and school support staff, such as school psychologists and school social workers. It also calls for the early involvement of parents and other family members and for the swift and progressive involvement of such other layers as community agency personnel when problem resolution is not forthcoming. The interval between intervention steps should usually be one to two weeks, in contrast to the much longer intervals in prevailing school intervention practices. Through the use of the School Decision Chart, children can be identified early, the family can be involved within one week of problem identification, and new players can be added to the process weekly until a solution is reached. Steps in the intervention process should sometimes be skipped or repeated as practitioners become more familiar with how the model works best for them.

The steps of the School Decision Chart call for an increased teacher awareness and use of systems principles, earlier and more open involvement of families in school problem-solving efforts, the prompt and progressive assembling of larger groups of relevant "players," and the use of an ecosystems consultant in overall staff consultation and, particularly, in one- to three-session school-based

Figure 2.2. The School Decision Chart.

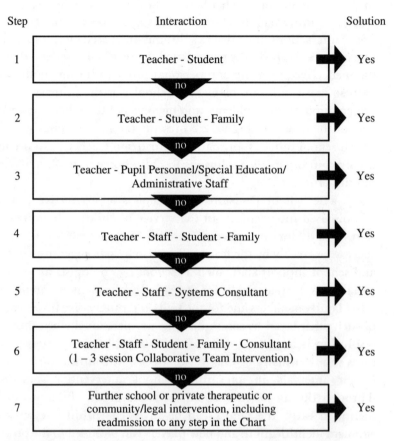

Step	Interaction	Solution
1	Teacher - Student	Yes
	no	
2	Teacher - Student - Family	Yes
	no	
3	Teacher - Pupil Personnel/Special Education/ Administrative Staff	Yes
	no	
4	Teacher - Staff - Student - Family	Yes
	no	
5	Teacher - Staff - Systems Consultant	Yes
	no	
6	Teacher - Staff - Student - Family - Consultant (1 – 3 session Collaborative Team Intervention)	Yes
	no	
7	Further school or private therapeutic or community/legal intervention, including readmission to any step in the Chart	Yes

Users of this chart can enter the sequence at any step and move up or down as needed. Time interval between steps is one to two weeks. Child problems can be identified by any member of the school staff but should be processed first by the child's primary teacher or case manager.

collaborative team interventions when school procedures are not succeeding.

Use of the Decision Chart with the Mother Who Was Labeled Incompetent

Step 1. Teacher Classroom Initiatives

In the case of Sharon Y.'s son Charles, when the problems first surfaced, the ecosystemically trained teacher would first attempt individual child management techniques, such as requesting Charles to sit still; asking what the matter was; and ascertaining whether he could see, hear, and understand the work. However, in my experience, individually based problems are not usually the primary reason that children have problems in school. This teacher-student interaction is Step 1 on the Decision Chart.

Step 2. The Teacher/Family Meeting

After several unsuccessful attempts over a week or so to solve Charles's school problem, the teacher would telephone Sharon, not only to report the child's behavior (and leave it up to the parent to cope independently with it) but also to invite both parents (in this case, Sharon and her current boyfriend) to a meeting with the teacher at school. The request to meet, and to involve both parents, is based on the ecosystemic belief that when a child is having problems in school, the most likely cause of the problem is parent-parent disagreement about child management, school-family disagreement about school behavior, parent-child conflict, marital problems, or other relationship issues in the ecosystem in which the child lives.

The ecosystemically trained teacher would want to discuss family matters in a collaborative fashion, with the child present, or possibly also alone with the parents, to assess what relationship issues might be relevant to the problem before recommending such intrapsychic procedures as individual testing, referral to specialized resource rooms, or other forms of special help in or out of school. If Charles's teacher had had such an open discussion with Sharon, very likely many family problems would have come to light—the drug addiction of Sharon's ex-husband, problems with her boyfriend, her own depression and unresolved grief, her child management problems, or other issues. The teacher would have offered support in the form of empathy, warmth, respect, genuineness, self-disclosure, and many other elements of good therapeutic communication that are available in the repertoire of the good teacher (Carkhuff, 1969). The teacher might have recommended family therapy, not individual therapy for the child.

Step 3. The School Strategy Meeting

After consulting with Sharon and her boyfriend, the teacher in the school-based ecosystemic collaboration model would do a number of things. First, she would increase her efforts to develop a close relationship with Charles, facilitate good relationships between Charles and his peers, initiate class discussion of divorce or death (Berger, Shoul, and Warschauer, 1992), or use other individual teacher techniques that can be very helpful in a case like this.

Second, the teacher would continue to reach out and be receptive to ongoing, frank, collaborative discussion with the child's mother and boyfriend regarding not only child issues but also adult issues at home.

Third, the teacher would consult with other staff members in the school, including the school social worker, the guidance counselor, and the principal, regarding further steps that might be taken to help Sharon and her family. At a meeting that should, preferably, include all the relevant school players, plans can be developed, for example, to coordinate with the school attended by Sharon's other child, to hold similar teacher-parent meetings and follow-up collaboration at the other school, to arrange a districtwide meeting of all school staff involved in the case without the family present (an extension of Step 3), or a school- or districtwide meeting with family present (the Step 4 format).

Step 4. The Family-School Meeting

A meeting involving school staff and the family, either on a school building level or a districtwide level, is necessary when individual teacher efforts, with or without staff consultation, are not working. Such a meeting would be scheduled approximately three to six weeks following the original presentation of the child problem. At this meeting, the teacher(s) would be assisted by school mental health professionals, school social workers, school psychologists and guidance counselors, for example, or by special education teachers, principals, and others who, because of their training and skill in ecosystemic collaboration (or other skills), can provide specialized perspectives on individual and family problems. At this meeting, the failure of current efforts can be admitted, and requests for new ideas and recommendations can be made. Usually, many people at these meetings have ideas. It is up to an ecosystemically trained leader of this meeting to orchestrate the interactions so that a solution is collaboratively decided upon and implemented. Conflicts between any of the players need to be resolved if any success is to be forthcoming. In the case of Sharon, disagreements between the "intrapsychic" and "contextual" contingents would have to be processed. If these conflicts are not fully resolved in one meeting, further meetings can be scheduled. The goal in Step 4 is to reach a consensus, or at least to reframe the problem as contextual adult disagreement rather than an individual child problem.

Step 5. The Consultant Strategy Meeting

If Step 4, whether through one or several meetings, is unsuccessful at resolving the child problems, it is time for the school system to bring in an ecosystemic consultant, external to the school, who is highly skilled in ecosystemic interventions and organizational, especially school, consulting. It is the consultant's job in Step 5 to engage the trust of relevant school staff, to correctly diagnose the child problem in an ecosystemic way, and to recommend an intervention plan that the school players support. Such an effort was described earlier in the case of Sharon.

Step 6. The Collaborative Team Intervention

The collaborative team intervention in Sharon's case has already been described. Intervention with other families might include a different cast of characters. The keys to the success of the intervention are group consensus and follow-up. Since conflict and disagreement between several players in the ecosystem is almost guaranteed when a problem reaches Step 6, the commitment of the school to get to the core of the problem, in whatever system or subsystem it may reside, is critical to success.

Step 7. Follow-Up

Follow-up in Sharon's case has already been described. Since this case is not completely resolved at the time of this writing, follow-up in the future will include a collaborative meeting early in the school year in the schools the boys attend. Continuing collaboration is planned among all other players involved.

Summary

The case study presented in this chapter is somewhat representative of the difficulties facing families, schools, and communities all over the United States. The operational mechanics of a school-based eco-systems collaboration model were detailed to show how such a case can be managed through use of the School Decision Chart, a flow-chart describing progressive school-based procedures in child problem solving. Chapter Three will provide further elaboration of the roles that can be played by family, school, and community agency players within the context of school-based ecosystemic collaboration.

3

LEADERSHIP
WITHIN
THE ECOSYSTEM

For the school-based ecosystems collaborative model to work, someone has to direct it; that is, someone has to identify the relevant
collaborators, assess their level of functioning, provide necessary
training to any collaborators who need it, conduct collaborative
team meetings when necessary, and monitor follow-up efforts. This
person—usually the ecosystemically trained school coordinator—
works under the supervision of the ecosystems consultant, assuming
progressively more numerous and complex functions. The consultant's job is to fill service delivery gaps, train staff, and conduct
collaborative team interventions and other meetings that the school
coordinator is not yet prepared to do. (The functioning of the ecosystems consultant was addressed in Chapters One and Two, and
more will be said about this role in Chapter Four.) In this chapter,
the collaborators in a school-based ecosystemic intervention will be
identified and briefly discussed, and specific guidelines will be
given for how the school coordinator, with the assistance of the

ecosystems consultant, can direct the collaborators through a successful effort and train them to eventually manage such an effort on their own.

The Collaborators

For the ecosystemic collaborative model of intervention to be optimally successful, it really should be a team effort of all the "collaborators," that is, the people whose actions can significantly affect the outcome of an ecosystemic intervention. Some good can be accomplished by the independent efforts of one or more collaborators, for example, a teacher or a parent, but the best results occur when an entire school district and consortium of community agencies adopt the collaborative model together.

Potential collaborators might be chosen from three general categories: family, school, and community. The number of people who might be relevant to the solution of a child's problem is potentially quite large. The child's mother and father and the child's regular classroom teacher are obviously very important characters. But other people, not traditionally involved in school interventions, might also be relevant, such as a neighbor of the family or a teacher from the child-care center. Exhibit 1 presents partial listings of likely collaborators. This list is by no means exhaustive. As practitioners begin thinking in an ecosystemic way, they can add to this list creatively as needed.

Family Players

The most important people to children are usually their parents and other extended family members. It is imperative that fathers and mothers become active members of collaborative teams designed to help children. Henderson (1987), Wolfendale (1986), and others have thoroughly discussed the overwhelming influence of parent involvement on children's school performance. Other family members, siblings and grandparents, for example, are also important.

Parents

Both parents of the child with problems need to be involved in collaboration efforts. When children are having trouble, it is likely

Exhibit 3.1. Players in the Ecosystem.

Student	School	Community
Child	Teacher	Private therapist
Both biological	Principal	Juvenile court officer
parents	Assistant principal	Medical doctor
Siblings	Guidance counselor	Case worker, Depart-
Extended family	School psychologist	ment of Children
(aunts, uncles,	School social worker	and Youth Services
cousins,	Special teachers	Lawyer
grandparents)	Classroom aides	Town social worker
Stepfamily	Directors of special	Town youth officer
Adoptive family	services	Day-care worker
Friends	Teachers and support	Minister or other figure
Neighbors	staff of siblings	Police youth officer

that fathers and mothers are disagreeing about parenting or that marital problems are of considerable magnitude. Skilled observation of the interaction between mother and father usually results in an understanding of the cause of the child's problem. Later in this chapter, a list of questions will be provided that can be asked of parents and others to elicit their opinions and the specific disagreements between them. In cases where parents don't disagree, individual psychological problems of one or both of the parents can usually be identified, or other sources of stress, such as financial difficulties, may be causing a disturbance. Even divorced parents living in different states should be invited to collaborative meetings.

Fathers

Although all collaborators are important, fathers may be the most important. In traditional interaction between home and school, fathers are often left out or involved as vestigial appendages. Even interventions that are ecosystemic often do not involve fathers (for example, "Case Study of Larry," Fine, 1992, pp. 12–15). Engaging fathers in child problem solving enables helpers in the school and from other sites to see up close the often dysfunctional or strained dynamics in the marital or divorce relationship. It also enables helpers to more directly contribute to the healthy restructuring of the relationship between parents by helping the parents to get closer together (a better marriage) or to get further apart (divorce). A father may be a very destructive influence on his children or a very constructive one; in either case, engaging the father enables everyone involved to understand the family dynamics better and to affect the influence of the father in the family. Even fathers who are in prison or who have abandoned their children before their birth continue to have great influence on their children through stories about them and through images fabricated in children's minds.

Siblings

Siblings of problem children need to be part of problem-solving efforts. These siblings may have problems of their own, or they may say or do things in the session that will provide a key to the family issues that underlie the identified child's problem. An observation of a disruptive older sibling at a collaborative meeting, for example, might help to explain similar disruptive behavior in his younger brother. Or, in the case where all children are interrupting each other and/or their parents, a generalized pattern of family chaos might be noticed. If the siblings of a problem child are quite functional and well-mannered, however, collaborators will want to search for ways in which the problem child may have been "specially" protected, undercontrolled, and given excuses for misbehavior. Leaving the sibling out of the treatment of an identified problem child can result in having to treat the sibling later, after exhaustive efforts have been expended in the treatment of the first child. The number of ways in which siblings add to the power of collaborative intervention is quite large.

Grandparents

Grandparents are sometimes invited to collaborative sessions, especially when primary care mothers are living with them. Grandparents can be very helpful to mothers and fathers, who are their children, and to their grandchildren, but they can also be very destructive. It is not uncommon for grandparents who did not do a very good job raising their own children to become more functional at raising their grandchildren. But some grandparents are intrusive and jealous and seem to want to compete with their children for the love and loyalty of the grandchildren. Whatever may be a specific family's dynamics, grandparents are frequently helpful additions to collaborative intervention efforts.

Stepparents

Additional help to collaborative work is provided by stepparents. It is important to find out whether stepparents are playing supportive roles to their spouses, who are biological parents of the children with problems or, as is more likely the case, they are playing some dysfunctional role. One common dysfunction occurs when step-fathers or stepmothers take over the discipline of unmanageable children for their passive or discouraged spouses (the children's biological parents). Children in this situation rebel quite systematically against these stepparent "intruders" and angrily resist their control with statements like "You're not my real parent." Other times, stepparents are jealous of continued functional contact between their husband's or wife's ex-spouse and may attempt to sabotage that relationship. To solve child problems, stepparents generally need to take secondary, supportive positions, while angry, divorced biological parents work out their personal and child management problems.

Extended Family and Others

There are many other family members, neighbors, and friends who might be invited to help in collaborative efforts. A friend of an angry, mentally unstable mother might be able to get her to listen to suggestions from collaborators. This person might be able to serve as an effective mediator. Neighorhood kids who fight with or reject a problem child might participate in a session designed to help all the children bury the hatchet. Again, a male neighbor of an unruly child raised by his grandmother might become a surrogate father to the boy. Sometimes, collaborations with more peripheral players can be accomplished by phone.

The School Players

The School Coordinator

In the school-based ecosystems collaborative model, many players with a wide range of personalities and skills need to work together as a team. For this to occur, many factors need to be in place, but primary among them is the identification of a team leader, case manager, or school coordinator, who functions at the school and, preferably, district level.

The school coordinator of a school-based ecosystemic collaboration program is its most essential player. He or she is usually a school social worker, school psychologist, guidance counselor, school adjustment counselor, or special education teacher. It is the coordinator's job to receive referrals, set up and eventually conduct the collaborative meetings, and to maintain and facilitate communication with all parties involved. It is usually the school coordinator who first becomes interested in the collaborative model and who convinces his or her principal and central administration to use it on a pilot basis. It is essential for the school coordinator to be highly enthusiastic about the ecosystems model and to be a person who can cope well with the high levels of pressure and negativity that can at times emanate from any sector of the collaborative system.

Within the collaboration model, the school coordinator is likely to be the court of first and last resort for the regular classroom teacher and other collaborative players. The school coordinator very likely has more extensive training in systems thinking and procedures than anyone in the school and is most likely to offer good advice on how to relate to a student or a student's family in a helpful way.

Facilitating ecosystemic collaborative interventions is a new role for most school mental health professionals. Considerable training and administrative support are necessary for this transition to be successful (Conoley, 1987; Fine and Holt, 1983; Green and Fine, 1980).

The School Social Worker

As mentioned earlier, the school coordinator will most likely be the school social worker. Of all school employees, the school social worker works most closely with the family and the social system of the child. In current school practice, it is not unusual for the school social worker to call the parents of children who are experiencing socio-emotional or behavioral problems. School social workers are also used to making home visits to parents, usually without the child present. Through the adoption of an ecosystems collaborative approach, the school social worker can save time in family work by seeing the families in school. He or she can also expand the notion of family work to include the whole family, as well as share the responsibility for family work with the whole staff.

The Teacher

Another key player in the ecosystemic collaborative model is the regular classroom teacher. It is this person who works with the child every day and observes the child's behavior most closely. High school teachers observe students for shorter periods of time, but they have greater opportunities to observe more students than do classroom teachers in the lower grades. It is not an exaggeration to say that some teachers are, in many ways, surrogate or substitute parents. These teachers may choose to be distant and uncommunicative with the students' families, or close and involved. For the collaborative model to work, regular classroom teachers must be willing to accept their "frontline" role in regard to students' social and emotional needs as well as to students' abilities to learn math or English.

Teachers must like and love children and be willing to get involved with them and their families. They must understand that sending a problem child to social workers, school psychologists, school counselors, special education teachers, administrators, and outside therapists should only be done as a support to a teacher who has already done his or her best to communicate with a child about any difficulty the child may be having in class or about unacceptable attitudes the child may be displaying. They should understand that to send a child out of class for counseling, punishment, or "special" education may be to reject the child in a way akin to sending a child out of a home. They should understand that it doesn't make sense to expect social workers or school counselors to develop relationships with hundreds of children in the artificial setting of a school office when they, the teachers, already have great opportunities to do this on a day-to-day basis as part of their normal classroom activities.

There is certainly a place for social workers, administrators, and the like in schools. But my experiences have taught me that one of the most destructive school practices of our day is the labeling of children as somehow temporarily or permanently unacceptable for life in the regular classroom. Just as children can be, by and large, maintained in their biological homes, they can also be maintained in regular school classrooms. It is not that the children are deviant, but that the adults do not understand the primacy of systemic or contextual causes of—and solutions to—child problems.

The Principal

The principal is not usually the person who starts the collaborative program in a school, but he or she is vitally necessary to its success. The school principal must support the program from the beginning and defend the school coordinator against the negativity and sabotage of some school teachers, support staff, and parents. The principal needs to set the tone for the program and introduce the ecosystems consultant to the staff in a positive manner. It is this player who needs to demonstrate leadership by coming to collaborative meetings with or without the family and by setting an example of concern for the whole child and the child's family. Without leadership within the school building, the efforts of the school coordinator and ecosystems consultant will be dismissed by some staff members, much as siblings reject each other in family feuds. If schools are going to successfully adopt the reform required by the ecosystemic collaboration model, principals will have to lead the way.

The Special Education Teacher

Among the next most important players is the special education teacher. This person can be very helpful, or very oppositional, to the collaborative agenda. Many special educators have unfortunately been trained in a linear intrapsychic model to believe that most educational difficulties are caused by neurological and learning difficulties best treated by special attention. The position expressed in this book is quite different and calls for a different role for the special educator, one which supports systems concepts instead of intrapsychic ones. There are such things as legitimate educational needs of students, such as "gaps" in material that should have been learned previously, or extra help in certain areas of learning that are difficult for certain students. The wholesale labeling and warehousing of large populations of students in special environments is, however, unnecessary and abusive. A recent study reported that 17 percent of students in Massachusetts schools were labeled "special education" (Ribadeneira, 1991). Special educators can be helpful by learning systems concepts and helping families to understand the connection between dysfunctional parent-child relationships and difficulties in concentration. These professionals can also help regular classroom teachers with strategies for treating all children "specially" in the regular classroom. All children have special needs, because we are all different and special.

The School Psychologist

In traditional school settings the school psychologist is asked to test the individual student's intellectual and psychological functioning, to dispense such labels as learning disabled (LD) and emotionally disturbed (ED), and to make recommendations for special individual treatment. If a school psychologist becomes trained in systems thinking, he or she can learn to view a child's intellectual and psychological functioning within a family, school, and community context and to assess the whole system, not just the child. Carlson (1992) and Paget (1987) discuss numerous vehicles for family and systems assessment.

    As was mentioned previously, although school psychologists apparently recognize the need for systems approaches, they continue to work primarily from a linear, individual perspective (Carlson and Sincavage, 1987). "Systems" assessments can be conducted through formal family assessment instruments or through informal individual and group interviews of family, school, and community personnel (Friedman, 1969). The collaborative team intervention (CTI), Step 6 in the School Decision Chart, is an excellent format for systems assessments. The school psychologist may also be the school coordinator for the collaboration program.

The School Counselor

It is the job of the school counselor to help individual students with their academic, vocational, and personal interests and problems, as well as to provide group education to classes on various educational topics. Through training in systems thinking this person can counsel and present material in a way that takes into account the powerful impact on children of the relationships in families and schools. It is the appreciation of the importance of the system around the child that will stimulate the school counselor to talk to the parents and other relevant adult figures about the child's problems and to understand that children are less interested in confidentiality and privacy than in improving relationships with others. After receiving confidential information from students and others, the school counselor can secure the necessary permissions to facilitate communication and discussion with those involved in the child problem about issues that are the most significant obstacles to educational and personal progress. The school counselor may also be the school coordinator for the collaboration program.

Central Administration

A significant collaborative role is played by central administration personnel, for example, the superintendent of schools, the director of special education (SPED), and the director of pupil personnel services (PPS). Just as the principal provides leadership for regular teachers and others in the school building, the central administration provides parallel leadership for principals and specialists, for example, social workers and special education teachers, who report to central authorities. For an ecosystemic collaboration program to have the power to operate and thrive, authority must be vested in it from the top of the system's hierarchy. In addition, complaints that will inevitably be generated by an effort to change a system must be received and understood by the executives of the system in a way that protects the program and its staff.

Other School Staff

There are many other potential collaborators among school staff, for example, the school nurse or special in-school tutors. The student body of a New Hampshire high school recently petitioned its administrators to allow the two school custodians to give the valedictory address (Baker, 1991). The administration resisted vehemently, but the student body was adamant because of the popularity of these two men. The student body prevailed, and the custodians gave the address. Any person on a school staff and any student in a school is a potential "collaborator" in ecosystemic intervention.

The Community Players

The cooperation of community players—workers in the police department; the Department of Child and Youth Services (DCYS); and the superior court, juvenile matters branch (SCJM)—is vital to the collaboration program. Officers of these organizations can be helpful in so many ways. In the case of Sharon Y., it was the youth officer who suggested that the school refer the family to the consultant for private family therapy. These organizations can be involved to various degrees, from informal requests and relationship building to formal commitment by the organization. Community partnerships or coalitions can also be created in which the directors of the various community agencies pledge their support of collaborative efforts. However it is arranged, the cooperation of community collaborators needs to be secured.

Various community workers and personnel can be invited to participate in collaborative efforts. Probation or youth officers are frequently invited to help in the motivation of those youths already implicated in illegal activity. Child protection workers may be invited when abuse charges have been filed against parents. Private therapists already working with a particular child or family can be invited. The goals of inviting personnel outside the family and school include the following:

1. The coordination of work. It is often the case with children
    with school problems that several agencies and people are
    working separately or at cross-purposes. In a collaborative for-
    mat, agency triangles are easier to handle (Carl and Jurkovic,
    1983).
2. An increase in leverage with a child or family. Each person
    involved with a child has a different relationship and type of
    influence on that child. Where one person, for example, a prin-
    cipal, may not have much influence on a student, a court officer
    may.
3. An opportunity for everyone to learn from each other. The
    school and the ecosystemic consultant, for example, hope to
    learn more about the workings of the larger system and also to
    influence its use of ecosystemic principles and procedures.

The Youth Officer

Most towns and cities have youth officers who are usually police
officers on special assignment to work with youth. These officers
can be very helpful to the collaborative effort by talking privately
to students and families at their homes or in school about a student's misbehavior. The youth officer can be encouraging and
friendly or threatening and punitive, as needed. He or she can educate student, family, and school staff about the legal consequences
of continued misbehavior by the student. This officer can also help
a mother to secure a restraining order against an abusive husband
and even drive the mother to the court from a school meeting in
which this problem has been identified. The youth officer is an
invaluable player in collaborative efforts with disruptive, out-of-
control children.

The Workers from the Department
of Child and Youth Services (DCYS)

Most state laws decree that the Department of Child and Youth
Services be contacted when there is suspicion of child abuse by a
parent or guardian. In a collaborative intervention format, the
DCYS worker can benefit from hearing the many testimonies given

at collaborative school meetings, as opposed to following the traditional format of one-to-one interviews. This worker can also refer a case to the school collaborative team when the case is identified by someone outside the school, and can also become part of the school-based collaborative team.

The Probation Officer

The officer of the superior court, juvenile matters branch, or more simply, the probation officer, can have a very positive effect on collaborative efforts. Whereas a child may not believe a parent, school official, or town youth officer who warns the child about the legal consequences of misbehavior, the court officer has delegated power to remove the child from the home and school and to place this child in a foster home or residential treatment facility. The participation of this officer in collaborative meetings gives the family and school more leverage with a child and serves to offset more serious challenges to authority by the child.

Private and Public Therapists and Other Community Support

Despite the best collaborative efforts in school, many families of children experiencing home and school difficulties will need additional help outside of school. This help might be needed from family therapists in the private or public sector or from other social agencies like the Department of Income Maintenance, the Camp Fire Kids, or the Big Brothers/Big Sisters organization. It is the job of the school coordinator of the collaborative program to invite whoever might be helpful to become a member of a collaborative team.

Directing the Players Through the Collaborative Team Intervention

Engagement Stage

Identifying and communicating with the relevant characters in a child's life is a major part of the ecosystemic collaborative effort.

The collaborative team intervention provides an excellent opportunity to observe and affect the interactions of the important players in a child's life.

After listening to everyone's comments in the case of Sharon Y., the consultant first attempted to lower participants' resistance to what he knew from past experience and current observation would be, for some, a controversial analysis. After all, the analysis would be ecosystemic and interactive, and it would reframe a child problem as a systems problem. For the child to improve, everyone, not just the child, would have to change. The consultant apologized to the group in advance for any discomfort he may cause them, since he knew that not everyone had invited him. He also stressed that he was giving his opinion, which participants were free to adopt or discard, in whole or in part. He asked for the group's permission to continue.

Second, he asked those present if they all thought the children in the case had a problem. He apologized for this apparently stupid question and explained that some people, for example, one of the parents, may not think that the children had any problems. Both parents and the others involved need to agree that a child has a problem before a solution can be arranged. He told the story of a father in one collaboration session who thought that his nine-year-old son did not have a problem because even though he refused to do homework or pay attention in school, he already knew how to read and write better than the father did, and that was all the schooling he or his son needed.

Third, the consultant asked those assembled if they knew what the problem was, or what the solution to the problem was. Most of the opinions given about the child's problem in these sessions may very well be incorrect or secondary to the primary problem. Diagnoses currently held by participants will usually involve intrapsychic or neurological judgments, such as that the child is lazy, hyperactive, can't pay attention, or is sneaky. Very few opinions will be interactional (for example, that the child is angry at someone) or systemic (for example, that the child is playing a role in a larger family or school pattern).

The consultant needs to help the group assembled to accept a diagnosis of the problem that can lead to a solution. If a child is angry at his or her parents, it is possible to find out why and help parents and child to resolve their differences. If an angry child is treated with medication for hyperactivity that is really disguised anger, it is more difficult to solve the problem. In the session with Sharon, diagnoses had already been given that ranged from depression to learning disabilities. Few diagnoses were interactive. Solutions were similarly intrapsychic and included hyperactivity medication, special education, and hospitalization. Members of the group answered the consultant's question by admitting that they weren't certain of the problem, diagnosis, or solution. Finally, the consultant asked for a statement of the level of the group's motivation to solve the problem and again asked the group's permission to continue.

Analysis and Intervention Stage

After warning the group of the upcoming controversial analysis, the consultant sought to secure the group members' agreement that the children had a problem, their commitment to solving the problem, and their openness to hearing alternative solutions. After doing so, he diagnosed the problem as an ecosystemic deficit disorder (EDD), in which there were deficits in the functioning of relationships in the systems and subsystems of family, school, and community. The family-school relationship he defined as antagonistic, adversarial, and at various times competitive, avoidant, or merged (Power and Bartholomew, 1987). He noted that the school had referred the family to DCYS several times, that the mother and some of the school staff had disagreed regarding the nature of the child problem, and that opinions differed among the school staff, which qualified as school-school relationship problems. The consultant also noted parent-child conflict. He mentioned many instances of child misbehavior in the session and observed that efforts by the mother to make her sons sit still and cooperate were generally unsuccessful.

Finally, he wondered aloud what other conflicts there might be between or among other players in the room or out of the room. He suggested that until all the players could "get on the same wave length," it would be difficult to solve the child problems. Before the meeting ended, the consultant provided some advice on child management techniques (discussed in Chapters Five and Six of this book), made suggestions for alternative school labeling and handling of the children, offered his continued availability for further consultation, and strongly suggested that the family get involved in family therapy. He, of course, also recommended continuing family-school collaboration.

The collaborative team intervention format described above was intended to accomplish a number of goals:

1. To reframe the child problem as an ecosystemic one
2. To note specific examples of ecosystemic conflicts and issues observable in the present situation
3. To support the mother, who was seen as incompetent and the villain of the piece by most school staff
4. To open the school staff to looking in the mirror and entertaining the possibility of working together from a different perspective of child problem causality and resolution

While not a perfect or complete model for accomplishing these goals, the collaborative team intervention covers most of the territory they outline and sets a lot of positively reverberating wheels in motion.

Summary

Identifying and communicating with the significant people in a child's life is a major part of the ecosystemic collaborative effort. The collaborative team intervention provides an excellent forum for these people to meet and to observe and affect each other's interactions as they influence the child. This chapter lists most of the major characters likely to be involved in an ecosystemic collaborative effort to solve a child's problems; however, such lists will differ for each separate case. The school coordinator and the ecosystems consultant, with the support of the school principal, play vital complementary roles in directing the collaboration so that it develops in a positive way. Case studies presented in the chapters that follow will contain additional examples of the ways in which leaders of ecosystemic collaborative interventions can organize and positively restructure the interactions and patterns of the child's ecosystem.

4

THE IMPORTANCE
OF
DIRECT COMMUNICATION

As we have already seen, the role of the consultant in school-based ecosystems collaboration is extremely important, since it is he or she who brings the expertise in this model into the school system. In many ways, this role is different from traditional consultant roles (Caplan, 1970; Gallessich, 1982; Fisher, 1986; Martin, 1983), although the ecosystems consultant will at times be called upon to perform traditional consultation roles, for example, mental health consultation (Caplan, 1970), behavioral consultation (Bergan, 1977), or systems consultation (Wynne, McDaniel, and Weber, 1986). Working within the collaborative model, however, the ecosystems consultant may be called upon to perform two or more of these roles simultaneously, for example, to be consulting at the same time on classroom management of children, administrative style of the principal, parenting strategies, family-school relationship patterns, or marital problems of the parents.

Further, although traditional models differ in the content of the consultation (for example, theme interference, behavioral management, or circular transactions), they do generally have in common a number of process characteristics—for example, a one-to-one relationship between a consultant and consultee; a focus on the consultee's relationship with a third party, known as a client; and a confidential relationship between the consultant and the consultee; as well as other factors (Erchul and Conoley, 1991). In school-based ecosystems collaboration, it may be necessary to modify a traditional consultation role because of the collaborative context, for example, to sacrifice the confidentiality among the consultee and client collaborators because of the need to give an opinion with both the consultee and client present in the same room.

Finally, within school-based ecosystems collaboration, it is difficult to distinguish between consultee and client, or between consultant and collaborator, because these roles are continually shifting in a context of partnership. As is probably clear by now, participants' boundaries in collaborative relationships become diffuse. Fine (1992) observes that "systems-ecological" interventions call for "a modification of the model of consultation that depicts the consultant as an outsider with clear-cut boundaries between his or her involvement and the consultee's ownership of the problem" (p. 12).

Because of the above considerations, the effective ecosystems consultant must be someone capable of functioning fluidly in a spontaneous and somewhat unpredictable atmosphere. Many collaborative team intervention sessions are emotionally charged, and there may only be one such meeting, since there is no guarantee that participants will return for a second session. The consultant will not usually have the luxury of a leisurely conversation with a consultee at a distant time and place about what happened. These contingencies appear to require three primary assessment and intervention skills on the part of the ecosystems consultant: (1) the ability to quickly engage—that is, attract trust, respect, and affection from—participants; (2) the ability to make quick, accurate ecosystemic assessments; and (3) the ability to be direct in communication, that is, to speak honestly, though respectfully and supportively, with participants, even when voicing opinions that may disturb others or increase tension and hostility. An example might be the ability to ask participants to discuss embarrassing or sensitive topics and to commit themselves to immediate change in the ways they do things. Many other skills are, of course, essential, for example, patience, listening, and a large repertoire of facilitation and therapeutic skills.

A skill that includes or overlaps all three of the primary skills needed by the ecosystemic consultant is that of being direct. A consultant must be able to confront—and help others confront—the reality of a situation. Confrontation was one of a group of Carkhuff's "helping," or communication, skills, which also included empathy, warmth, respect, concreteness, genuineness, self-disclosure, and immediacy (Carkhuff, 1969). In my judgment, directness in communication is underutilized in private, clinic, and school-based intervention and consultation, and professional writing almost uniformly recommends tactics of indirectness and avoidance in school-based meetings; yet the use of directness can contribute significantly to participant change in brief, school-based, collaborative efforts. The discussion that follows focuses on how, in the process of being direct, the consultant can use a wide variety of interview skills, such as positive reframing, that are extremely valuable and fully compatible with a direct, as opposed to an indirect or avoidant, consultation style.

The Use of Indirectness in Current Practice

Many writings in the family-school collaboration literature recommend indirectness, protectiveness, and avoidance in dealing with family and school issues (Aponte, 1976; Eno, 1985; Foster, 1984; Kral, 1992; Power and Bartholomew, 1987), and many others simply report the use of indirect tactics with families and school personnel (for example, Fine, 1992; Kral, 1992; Okun, 1984). These writings generally discuss the use of strategic interventions, in which insight is not important, and through which clients, for example, children, parents, and teachers, improve without understanding why. The dictionary defines *strategy* as "the science of planning and directing large-scale military operations, specifically (as distinguished from 'tactics'), of maneuvering forces into the most advantageous position prior to actual engagement with the enemy; skill in using . . .

strategem." *Strategem* is defined as "a trick, scheme, or device used for deceiving an enemy in war; any trick or deception." Although there are other secondary dictionary definitions for strategy, including blueprint and plan, the first meaning of the word seems most applicable to some family-school interventions reported in the literature. The rationale for strategic, or indirect, intervention in schools is school rigidity and the high level of resistance to change that has been experienced by many investigators (Foster, 1984; Lightfoot, 1978). The use of blaming is particularly recommended against.

The problems with the indirect type of intervention are that it may not lead to prevention and education, two important goals of collaborative interventions, and that it may reinforce an expert-client, manipulative, or adversarial relationship, which is contrary to the goals of a collaborative model. Conoley (1987), for example, after describing three apparently effective strategic interventions with problem children, noted the following: "Obviously, this approach has some limitations. It is not an educative model. I doubt that people learned anything from the therapy they could verbalize to others or even to themselves. The focus on behavior change with no insight or instructions for generalization suggests strategic interventions have no preventive applications. They are meant, I think, to serve as temporary bridges, assisting families over particularly troublesome phases of family life. This contrasts with behavioral interventions that, while not demanding insight, are educational" (p. 483).

The failure of strategic interventions to generalize in clients' lives is evident in the "systems-ecological" intervention with a fifteen-year-old client called Larry, described by Fine (1992). Larry apparently received a couple of years of therapy while he was living in a group home, at which point consideration was given to moving him home to live with his biological mother. Larry chose not to move home. Fine comments: "By that time a younger brother had been identified by the parents as incorrigible and the family was once again in an uproar around that boy's problems. This seemed to be a replay of the mother's earlier experiences with Larry and signaled growing marital problems" (p. 14). In the intervention with Larry, which included many components, Fine reports using reframing as a "major technique" and spending a great deal of effort creating favorable "impressions" with teachers by using statements such as "we're in this together," and by suggesting that he saw the teachers as "victims" of Larry. By strategically engineering teacher allegiance, Fine was able to at least temporarily elicit their cooperation. But such methods, in my view, may not have empowered the teachers, family members, and other school officials to deal with Larry's brother or with the marital problems between Larry's mother and stepfather. Larry's brother and his stepfather were apparently not involved in the intervention with Larry. Furthermore, no mention was made in this intervention of Larry's biological father.

Many other writers recommend avoiding directness with teachers and parents. Foster notes the following: "If a covert disagreement becomes overt during [a family-school interview], as often happens, it needs to be settled. This may entail a recess to meet with parents separately to help them resolve their differences before continuing the negotiations with the teacher" (1984, p. 126). Foster also recommends at times arranging "a temporary severance of contact between home and school" to break a negative sequence between parents and teachers and "a time-limited commitment from each that they will not communicate with the other." In another section of the same work, Foster comments on having successfully avoided dealing with a teacher-counselor conflict: "This tactic avoided exposing the intensity of the negative feelings between the teacher and the counselor and thereby avoided the risk of the therapist's getting involved in directly working with the teacher and counselor as clients" (p. 133).

In several articles, Lusterman (1985, 1992) outlines an "ecosystemic" approach in which he "interdicts" communication between home and school and establishes himself as a "bridge," a "mediator," and a "temporary buffer zone" between home and school (Lusterman, 1985, pp. 24–25). He recommends conversations on the telephone instead of a family-school meeting to "avoid some of the hierarchy problems that can arise in a school-family meeting, where the principal might be threatened by the presence of an outside "expert," and consequently maintain a formal and bureaucratic stance that inhibits communication" (1992, p. 368).

Aponte (1976) provides more caution against therapeutic directness in the following comment: "A delicate issue requiring attention from the start is the relationship of the school to the clinic vis-a-vis the child and family. The teachers request the Clinic's help with their pupil, but do not expect to be treated as clients" (p. 304). In requesting a family-school interview, Aponte and his staff report that they assured the counselor at the school that "we considered the school as resources for solution, not as targets for blame" (p. 305). Hoffmann and Long (1969) and Carl and Jurkovic (1983), however, caution that the therapist who acts as "social broker" or "advocate" can disempower families and become too omnipotent a figure in family affairs—an observation with which I concur.

References to recommendations for the use of indirect tactics abound in the family-school literature. While there is certainly just cause to be wary of the obstacles to ecosystemic success represented by teacher and school resistance to change (see Chapter Eleven), I recommend a more direct, though respectful and supportive, approach for use in school-based ecosystemic collaboration for several reasons, including the following:

1.   One of the major goals of this model is to multiply the number of empowered caregivers and to create a collaborative spirit among them. By working strategically with school or family, one client at a time, the consultant may achieve temporary peace and success, but impede the spread of ecosystemic awareness and practice. Clients may improve more or less quickly with a more direct and collaborative approach, but they will improve, and—more important from the viewpoint of a school program—educators will learn how to reproduce the results without continued dependence on the consultant.

2.   Overprotection is one of the key dysfunctional caretaking errors made by adults in families and schools. By protecting staff, family, and others from each other, the consultant is modeling this caretaking error.

3.   Interdiction and strategizing are compatible with a traditional therapist-client or consultant-consultee relationship, but in a collaboration model, everyone is at times a therapist and consultant as well as a client and consultee. The communication is quite open in this model, and such consultant maneuvers as prescribing

the symptom are both obvious and unacceptable. Directness is most compatible with the collaborative format.

In contrast to indirect, strategic, tactical, protective, interdictive, and buffering approaches, I strongly recommend a direct and assertive one. In their coverage of the school's use of a family systems approach, Braden and Sherrard note that "a frank statement of how the school views the problem, and how this view differs from the family's perspective, often motivates the family to reassess their perspective," thereby promoting "disequilibrium and uncertainty" (1987, p. 517). Paget recommends "a spirit of explicitness" in family-school communication (1987, p. 431).

The therapy approach most consistent with my own is Andolfi's use of "systemic provocation" (Andolfi, Angelo, Menghi, and Nicolo-Corigliano, 1983; Wendt, 1992; Whitaker, 1975). Andolfi and his colleagues point out that the perception of the problem and the therapist-family relationship can be radically redefined by an intense and disorienting provocation to the entire family system. Wendt recounts Andolfi's explanation that "the therapist intrudes in a nonprotective manner and yet contains the suffering and pain of the family. If the therapist is too scared, too protective, or too positive, the family will only stabilize and prolong therapy" (1992, p. 317). Wendt further states Andolfi's belief that "the therapist then is often able to intrude to a level of discussion that the family cannot or is too embarrassed to discuss, or to provoke action that people do not want to take to create change. To clarify, intrusion means moving with support into levels of hesistancy, embarrassment, and discomfort because it is only at these levels that meaningful change can occur" (p. 319). Although Andolfi frequently uses toys as metaphors in his systemic provocations, in my experience there are many other ways to enact this approach.

The Use of Directness in Collaborative Team Interventions

Since the goal of the collaboration model is the training of all participants in ecosystemic thinking and practice, one of the consultant's roles is to provide education and training in all facets of the collaboration process. The consultant needs to model directness in the first encounters with school system representatives through a clear description of the ecosystemic viewpoint and an honest interaction about the specifics of its implementation in the school district. School personnel should not be "finessed" into thinking it is something less invasive and controversial than it is. Teachers, principals, or parents should similarly be spoken to honestly about adult dynamics underlying child problems. Explanations of child behavior emphasizing circularity and reciprocity can be used, as well as the positive reframing of any situation, but often, in my view, it is necessary to be very specific in identifying who in the system is interfering most with progress and what that person needs to do. It is not always possible to be direct without getting fired or alienating a particular constituency, but directness should remain a goal and be used whenever possible. The level of directness acceptable to a particular school or school system should be negotiated beforehand. Negotiating with school leaders is discussed in detail in Chapters Eleven and Twelve.

The consultant's use of directness in collaborative team interventions should be used as a model for other consultant-consultee interactions. Some of these procedures were described in the discussion of the collaborative team intervention with Sharon and her family in Chapters One and Two. The basic format is as follows:

1. *Open the forum.* Make sure that everyone assembled has a chance to give his or her opinion regarding the nature of the problem as well as its cause and solution. Encourage honesty.

2. *Model straightforward problem solving.* Give an honest appraisal of the situation, emphasizing solutions. This appraisal should first cover individual and dyadic assessment. Positive reframing is acceptable, even advised, but beating around the bush is not. For example, the primary responsibility of parents for causing and solving child misbehavior might be stated as follows:

> It is my [the consultant's] opinion that children's misbehavior is primarily the result of parenting and other child caretaking behavior, especially the over- or underuse of protection and control. In the case of parenting behavior, mistakes are not the parents' fault, because parents learn these behaviors from their parents and other adults, and so on across the genera-

tions. In addition, parents have many personal problems they have also "inherited" from their families of
origin. And, too, there is not enough parenting education for parents.

It is difficult to talk about responsibility without suggesting blame, which is not the point of this
discussion. Rather, the bottom line of this discussion
is that parents and other adults can solve child problems if they are willing to look in the mirror at themselves and examine the messages they give to children.

The reader will note that the consultant uses reframing in
blaming previous generations and lack of education for the present
problem, but states that responsibility for change still lies with the
people in the room. This is consistent with Dunst and Trivette's
(1987) research conclusion that effective empowerment of recipients
of help requires that they (the recipients) assume a high degree of
responsibility for change. Too often in traditional school meetings,
participants claim to be mystified by the causes of a child's problem,
and recommend tests, placements, or further meetings to avoid discussing their private opinions of causality.

3. *Ask direct questions and get direct answers.* The parents,
educators, and other participants need to discuss and agree on the
following points:

a. Is there a problem?
b. What is it?
c. How serious is it?
d. Do you have a solution?
e. Do you want a solution?
f. How much do you want a solution?
g. Are you willing to consider solutions that involve new ideas
and ways in which you, the adults, need to change?

After giving the above analysis to the collaborative group,
the consultant should ask the members of the group if they agree
with the analysis and approach to the situation and if they will let
the consultant proceed. Most members of collaborative groups do

agree with this approach. Some questions or concerns are occasionally raised, and the consultant can skillfully answer the questions
briefly or ask that a response be postponed until later in the discussion. A chalk-board or flip chart is extremely useful for drawing
genograms, three-generational family tree diagrams illustrating the
relationships of all the members of a family (Bowen, 1978) and
ecomaps, which describe both the interaction within each subsystem and the interaction between subsystems (Lusterman, 1992).
Such tools help participants conceptualize the problem and family-
school relationship patterns.

4. *Help the group distinguish between accurate and inac-
curate ideas.* Participants need to compare and contrast opinions
about the problem, its causes, and solutions that have been stated
in the meeting. The consultant needs to give honest reactions to
these opinions and be particularly clear about the incorrectness of
neurobiological, psychiatric, or addictive labeling that absolves the
participants of their involvement in the problem and their responsibilities for solving it. The direct approach recommended here is
different from "strategic" recommendations for further testing that
a consultant may give, not because they are necessary but to avoid
confrontation with parents or teachers. The direct approach also
differs from the strategic use of testing results to avoid confrontation
over necessary changes in parent management style. Kral (1992), for
example, requested psychoeducational testing "to know where the
limits were" and used the results to reframe parental undercontrol
as the child's "developmental need" (p. 335). Kral also recommended that parents use the child's progress at home as "ammuni-
tion" against a teacher who apparently held a negative opinion
toward the child. Kral gives numerous other examples of elaborate
reframing to ensure that neither teacher nor parents would feel any
responsibility for the problem.

While all of these interventions are clever and were apparently effective, the consultant using the direct approach recommended in this book would view them as beating around the bush
with clients and, in fact, as inefficient and counterproductive for a
school-based model. It would certainly be logical, for example, that
parents advised by a therapist to test their child at the first occurrence of a problem would turn to testing again when the same child

had further problems, or for a teacher to leave responsibility for child change in the future to parents who were successful prior to his or her involvement. Within the context of school-based responsibility for children, the consultant would probably confront directly, in a collaborative team meeting, both the teacher's and parent's adult mismanagement and parent-teacher triangling, and ask both parties to work it out together with the consultant's help. The consultant's comments and opinions would eventually be followed by a request for the opinions and comments of those involved.

5. *Confront other systems issues.* It is at this point in the discussion that systems problems that are more than dyadic should be dealt with. The more difficult the child problem, the more likely that adult disagreements and conflicts are sustaining the problem. These issues need to be identified clearly at the school meeting. The consultant should identify the conflicts he or she sees and ask the members of the group for confirmation of his or her hypotheses. If parent-parent disagreements have been identified, the consultant will ask the parents to admit and talk out their differences. The consultant will point out the value in the viewpoints of both parents, but will also explain the inadequacies of each of their approaches. The general atmosphere will be informed by the consultant's statement that there must be a good reason for a child to have two parents.

The consultant also needs to be direct if marital problems, conflict between ex-spouses, or conflict between step-families become evident during the meeting. The consultant should make observations about these conflicts and again ask for confirmation. He or she should ask if participants realize the effect of these conflicts on the child, and if they are willing to work on resolving these conflicts. Family-school conflicts should be handled in a simliar way. The essential ingredients in these interventions are the willingness and ability of the consultant to get to the core of the child's problem, to state his or her opinions clearly, to ask the players involved in conflicts to work on them in the collaborative format, and to effectively facilitate conflict resolution.

6. *Recommend "experiments" for change.* Experiments should proceed from agreements made by all those present and

should be one or two weeks in duration. Asking people to directly and immediately change their ways—no matter how long the patterns may have been present—is accepted by most people.

The Mother Who Seemed Overprotective

An example of the use of consultant directness is available in the case of Kathryn, a mother who was overprotective regarding her eleven-year-old son's misbehavior in class. This boy had been a disruptive student for several years, but the mother had always defended him against his teachers. In a collaborative team intervention, it became evident that Kathryn's husband was more strict in his parenting approach than she was and that he agreed with the teacher's perspective. The task for the consultant was to be honest with the parents about their conflict in a way that would not alienate them and cause them to drop out of the collaborative process. To accomplish this task, the consultant used the six-step process just described. Of particular help were the questions listed in Step 2, since they elicited from the more resistant mother the admission that she very much wanted an answer to her son's problem and that her protective approach was not helping to solve the problem. With these points established, the consultant was able to work with the mother on her overprotective style. Similarly, the consultant was able to identify the father's tendency to underprotect his child in response to his wife's overprotectiveness. The parents were asked to deal with their conflict in the collaborative session, and the mother revealed that she was not well treated as a child and wanted to make things better for her son. She also admitted having felt a lack of control of her life as a child and an exaggerated need to win control battles with her husband. Through continued discussion, the mother did agree that her son's teachers were not abusive, as her own mother had been, and that she should support the teachers' efforts to make her son behave. Both parents agreed to an experiment in which a daily report card would be sent home indicating their son's grades in all his lessons and on such behaviors as conduct, effort, class participation, and homework. The parents were to provide the negative home consequence of time on the bed for unsatisfactory grades and the positive consequence of free time for satisfactory grades, at the rate of fifteen minutes per grade.

The results of this experiment were extremely good. Kathryn's son showed an immediate turnaround in school, a result that was maintained for the remainder of the school year (six months). The parents continued in marital therapy, even though the father had previously been unwilling to pursue therapy for more than one or two sessions because of his wife's inflexibility on the child-rearing issue. The teachers' attitudes toward the boy and his parents became much more positive, and family-school communication improved significantly. A major contribution to this improvement was the teachers' ability to understand their student's problem within the context of his mother's personal and family-of-origin issues and his parents' conflict with each other.

Supportive directness is clearly crucial in collaborative team interventions. Directness is also important in other school interactions. Chapters Seven through Ten describe collaborative team interventions that will further clarify the use of this approach as well as several other consultant skills.

Summary

Within the context of a school-based ecosystemic collaboration program the behavior of the school consultant differs from that in traditional consultation models in several ways. For example, it requires such consultant procedures as ecosystemic assessment skill, engagement, and directness. Directness is essential in collaborative intervention, and the ways in which it contrasts with more indirect, strategic, or avoidant techniques presented in the literature are significant.

Part Two

EDUCATING THE PLAYERS

5

ASSESSMENT SKILLS
FOR COLLABORATORS

Facilitating communication and cooperation among the relevant players in a child's life is essential to the task of raising and educating children. But those who communicate and cooperate must also know how to do their job. Discussion in the next two chapters will focus on training collaborators, mainly parents and teachers, in understanding the behavior of children and in methods by which adult managers can raise healthy, responsible, self-motivated children. Within the school-based ecosystems collaborative model, it is the school's job, through the expertise of the school coordinator and the ecosystems consultant, to train collaborators in assessment and intervention skills. As mentioned in Chapter One, child problem behavior may be interpreted from an individual, interpersonal, systemic, ecosystemic, or school-based collaborative point of view. Within the systemic analysis, the mesosystemic perspective (Bronfenbrenner, 1979) is particularly important to the collaborative model because it deals with interactions between systems, for example, between parents and and school personnel. Fine (1992) notes that "there is no standard operating procedure for a systems-ecological perspective" (p. 9). All of these perspectives can be subsumed under the general rubric of ecosystems.

Individual Assessment

From the individual perspective, what an adult perceives as a child problem may simply be the expression of a personality style that the child "inherited" or learned in the family—for example, assertiveness. Or it may be a characteristic common to all children, for example, a desire to experiment or accomplish. Also, a child whose every wish was granted in infancy may not easily give up this power when his or her parents insist on greater independence. In addition, an indulged child may have understandable difficulty adapting to normal developmental tasks or changes in family life, such as moving to a new house. Finally, from a physical or medical point of view, a child may have legitimate problems—an early childhood hernia, measles, chicken pox, or flu, for example. A controversial consideration under this individual category of assessment is the alleged presence of neurological symptoms or characteristics that are referred to in medical, psychological, and educational circles as hyperactivity, attention deficit hyperactivity disorder (ADHD), developmental disorders, neurobiological disorders, predisposition to alcoholism, and the like. Although adult managers of children need to focus in a linear way on individual characteristics and needs that have little to do with interactions with adults and everything to do with childrens' own individual organisms, it is my opinion that most child educational and home management problems are not primarily related to individual and intrapsychic factors, but rather to relational factors, to be covered in subsequent sections of this chapter.

Excuse Psychology

The ways in which parents, educators, and other adults deal with supposedly individual and neurological issues is extremely important in determining the success of parental, educational, and psychological efforts with children and is a matter that deserves extensive discussion because of the large number of children currently diagnosed with these problems. "Excuse psychology" is a way of thinking about children that attributes such problems as disruptive behavior or academic difficulty to causes beyond the control of the child. The causes are usually thought to be inside the child, for example, learning disabilities, attention deficit disorder (ADD), hyperactivity, or such other neurological or medical problems as allergies or sensitivity to sugar. Sometimes these causes are considered to begin outside the child, but they end up inside the child—malnutrition by neglectful parents during the first year of life, for example, or the emotional effects on the child of the parents' divorce. Whatever may be the real or imagined causes of a child's home or school problems, through excuse psychology, the child begins to be "understood" by adults, given "special" treatment, and provided a mortgage plan by which expectations of appropriate behavior are "laid away" to a future, somehow more manageable, time. Individual therapy, psychological testing, medication, and hospitalization are four of the key features of this "diagnostic layaway plan." Unfortunately, many individual and "special" childhood diagnoses do not result in solutions, and the "payment" for these mistakes eventually becomes two, three, or ten times greater because of the "interest" incurred by the child's stronger dysfunction in academic and behavioral habits. Developmental maturing helps with few of these problems, and the result after several years of "expert" incorrect diagnosis, is the correct identification of a problem that finally has become a behavioral problem—one that is in the child and is much more difficult to manage. Many examples of the diagnostic layaway phenomenon are provided throughout this book.

It probably must remain a mystery—or at least a matter of speculation—why attention deficit disorder and other diagnostic categories have become so popular. It is difficult to determine if children today are any more hyperactive or distractible than in the past. As with many other statistics—for example, those on crime—the main change may not be in the phenomenon but in the reporting. ADD and other neurological-educational-medical diagnoses seem to have replaced the equally intrapsychic, remote, and untreatable mental illness diagnoses of the past. Thomas Szasz (1961) has referred to these mental illnesses as "myths," and a similar follow-up book on "neuroedumedical" myths seems to be needed for this generation. Stanton Peele, writing about alcohol abuse, refers to this phenomenon as the "diseasing of America" (Peele, 1989). As with child mental diagnoses, neuroedumedical diagnoses afford the adult world the ability to distance itself from the child's problems and provide it with medication, testing, and special services that do not involve changes in such adult socioeconomic and political systems as families, schools, and professional services.

In addition to LD, ADD, and other problems of an allegedly neurological or educational nature, child problems have been attributed to many other pseudocauses, for example, poverty, prejudice, divorce, the absence of fathers, and other significant factors. But these are conditions, not causes. Many poor children, victims of prejudice, father absence, and other conditions, have been known to cope and succeed. Some handicapped artists, for example, born with no hands, learn to paint with their feet, and some born without hands or feet learn to hold their paintbrush with their mouths. Clarence Thomas, a recent appointee to the Supreme Court, spoke of refusing to use his poor Georgia background as an excuse for the inability to achieve. Children achieve primarily because of adults who care, take charge, and behave as competent child managers. Turning the corner on today's child crisis requires clarity of thinking about causes and cures. Only in this way can our limited resources of time and money produce successful outcomes.

It is important, at this juncture, to remember that, social and familial factors notwithstanding, children do experience difficulties that are neurologically, medically, and educationally based. There certainly are such things as learning differences, and even disabilities. Visual-motor difficulties and reading problems, for example, dyslexia, all deserve compensatory assistance from regular and special education personnel. It is nonetheless essential to avoid the prevailing pat reaction to child problems, which is to assume that the difficulty lies inside the child. Intrapsychic diagnoses lead to intrapsychic treatment strategies like educational and psychological testing; individual, group, and peer counseling in schools; referral for "outside" individual counseling with a private or agency therapist; referral to a pediatrician, neurologist, allergist, nutritionist, or other medical specialist; use of drugs like Ritalin and Dexedrine; or referral for "special" education or a placement outside the regular school, perhaps in a hospital or special school. In my experience, most of the problems that lead to any of the above referrals and actions do not stem from neurological, medical, or educational causes, but rather from flawed systemic interactions between parent and child, parent and parent, parents and school personnel, or among the personnel in the school. If it is true—as indeed it seems to be—that child home and school problems are caused mainly by interactions involving adults, then it becomes extremely important to question why adults are not the focus of assessment, diagnosis, and treatment. At the very least, it is important to look into possible systemic causes of child problems before enacting treatment based exclusively on intrapsychic or intrasomatic causes.

Motivational Deficit Disorder

Most child problems can be conceptualized as the result of caretaking dysfunctions, specifically a lack of balance in the control and protection of children. Overcontrol and undercontrol and overprotection and underprotection lead to various child problems, including a condition that I have termed motivational deficit disorder, or MDD. MDD is a state of undermotivation in which a child is either discouraged, spoiled, or otherwise detached from functional, cooperative, and creative behavior.

The concept of motivational deficit disorder can be viewed as an optimistic alternative to what might be called the misdiagnoses of attention deficit disorder (ADD), learning disability (LD), and other Ds (disorders, disabilities, deficits, diseases) that seem to be sweeping the nation. My use of the word "misdiagnoses" is, again, not designed to deny the existence of attention or learning difficulties. Rather, I use it to dispute what seems to be an overstated power of these "disorders" to interfere with learning and to cause misbehavior. ADD diagnosticians are guilty of circular reasoning when they observe attention difficulties, label them a "disorder," and then attribute the attention difficulties to the disorder.

Another violation of logic is the prescription of medication for the treatment of ADD. Ritalin, Dexedrine, Phenobarbitol, and

other drugs used to treat attention deficit disorder and hyperactivity
will produce effects, sometimes quieting. After all, they are drugs.
The occasional effectiveness of a drug, however, does not prove the
existence of the disorder, since it is possible, for example, that the
same drug could affect any non-ADD person in similar ways. The
drugs have also been known to produce negative side effects; for
example, sleep, eating, and growth problems have been reported
following the use of various medications.

In my experience, most children who are diagnosed with
ADD or as hyperactive and given Ritalin or Dexedrine can become
manageable and calm without medication in response to changes
in parent or caretaker behavior. Purveyors of the "D" words are,
unfortunately and inadvertently, discouraging children and adults
from taking responsibility for their own behavior and are offering
society "diagnostic layaway plans" in which problem behavior is
attributed to mysterious causes and in which solutions are either not
achievable or are someone else's responsibility. These plans have to
be paid off later at high interest rates, for example, through the
incarceration or placement in rehabilitation facilities of people
whose problems were much more manageable in their original
form. The main result of diagnostic layaway is, of course, motivational deficit disorder, in which children and parents are undermotivated to achieve because of a belief that the disability or disease
prevents them from doing so.

Parent Training Deficit Disorder

Overemphasizing ADD, LD, and other problems such as economic
disadvantage, usually leads to overprotection and undercontrol of
children, which produces motivational deficits. Motivational deficits can also be caused by parents who overcontrol or underprotect
their children, expect too much from them, and insist on scheduling
their lives, including when to go to bed, get up, and do their homework. These are the "Great Santini" parents, after the fictional
character, who expect their children to salute when they go by and
grow up to be president of the United States. From early ages, children need to learn progressive self-regulation skills, and caretakers
who interfere with this process are, again, asking for diagnostic

layaway plans in which children are called "bad seeds," "like this from birth," and blamed for problems the caretakers create. All of these caretaker control and protection disorders can be categorized within the family as parent training deficit disorder (PTDD), and within the school and community as adult management deficit disorder (AMDD). By shifting the "D" diagnoses to the adult world, we shift the focus to the adults who caused the problem instead of the children who are the diagnostic victims. This leads to a second level of assessment.

Dyadic Assessment

Dyadic assessment evaluates the interaction between two people in a dyad, for example, the relationship between a mother and her child. Although children's lives are embedded in systems larger than the mother-child, father-child, or teacher-child relationships, these relationships are the most important, and should be the main focus of efforts to work with problem children. The two major dimensions of adult caretaking behavior are those of protection and control. *Protection* is defined as "an act of shielding from injury, danger, or loss; guarding, defending." Protecting children from danger is obviously a key variable in raising children. Failure to protect children can result in physical damage, ranging from simple bruising to maiming. Or it can result in psychological damage, for example, a loss of confidence or self-esteem. There is also a possibility of overprotection, however—a less obvious caretaking mistake—which can be equally devastating for children by depriving them of the challenge of coping with difficult situations in life which they are capable of handling. Successful parenting or adult caretaking requires a balanced approach to protecting children, in which they are allowed and encouraged to do whatever they are capable of doing and shielded only from that which they cannot manage safely.

Control, the other major parenting function, is defined as "a checking or verifying activity against a standard or duplicate." Secondary meanings of *control* are "exercising authority over, regulating, directing, commanding, curbing, or restraining." All of these meanings are important for the adult caretakers of children. Directing and restraining a child should only be done when the child is not conforming to a standard on his or her own (that is, self-regulating or self-directing). The standards to which children are expected to conform are idiosyncratic standards within each family, school, neighborhood, and the like, but these standards are also influenced by the larger cultural factors of race, religion, socioeconomic group, and other factors. Control is extremely important in bringing up children because it ensures that children will follow rules of behavior that will result in successful and productive habits in the present and future. Control, like protection, can be overdone or underdone. Overcontrolling parents are too rigid and allow too little freedom for children to experiment with autonomy and separation. These children can become narrow in their thinking if they comply, and angry and rebellious if they don't. Undercontrolling caretakers allow too much freedom and thereby help to create chaotic, disorganized children. Adult caretakers need to use control in a balanced way that allows children to experiment within flexible and reasonable limits that will accommodate the changing times and customs of the larger culture.

Universe of Parent and Child Behavior

Successful parenting or child caretaking should lead to a state of "automatic pilot" behavior or self-regulation in children. In this state of mind, the child makes generally good decisions without parental interference and asks for help only when he or she needs it. Parents attend from an appropriate distance and intervene, preferably by asking questions, only when necessary. "Parenting by questions" is a powerful regulation device that is described fully in Chapter Six. It stresses assessing children's wishes and ability to take care of themselves before the parent invokes the use of external protection or control. When a child has never developed self-regulation or has disengaged from it, caretakers need to provide either more or less control or protection to develop or reengage it. An infinite variety of parenting and child behavior styles or patterns are created by relationships between two dimensions of parenting behavior, namely, protection and control, and two dimensions of child behavior, flexibility and attachment.

The pattern of behavior that parents use will have significant direct effects on the behaviors their children adopt. Although the parent-child relationship is clearly influenced by the behavior of the child as an individual, by the reciprocal interaction of the parent and the child, and by many other factors, the preeminent influence is the behavior of adults—principally parents. The behavior of adults is, similarly, influenced by, and even formed in response to, the parenting behavior of their parents.

We can identify four varieties of dysfunctional parenting styles that relate fairly directly to four dysfunctional child behavior styles (see Figure 5.1). Although this analysis is somewhat linear and more limited than a larger total systems analysis would be, it illustrates the counter influences of control and flexibility, and protectiveness and attachment between parent and child.

The Overprotective, Undercontrolling Parent

The overprotective and undercontrolling parent will attempt to mediate excessively between the child and the environment so that the child is never hurt. This parent will also let the child "get away with murder," so that it is not "traumatized" or hurt by the parent's expectations. Children raised in this dysfunctional style are deprived of experiencing real physical and social boundaries and, as a result, doubt their own abilities. Such children simultaneously believe that they are invincible and in charge of the world, and they become "spoiled brats" or "child terrorists" who are disrespectful, disobedient, and physically aggressive. These children are the "chaotic-enmeshed" children in Figure 5.1. As a result of adult undercontrol, these children become *chaotic,* that is, confused, disorganized, and overly responsive to any stimuli. They have not been taught to pursue goals, delay gratification, or tolerate frustration. They rush aimlessly from one activity to another while their caretakers provide little direction, control, or supervision. In addition, as a result of adult overprotection, these children are *enmeshed,* that is, entangled or caught up in relationships with their adult caretakers to the point where they have no mind of their own, no identity, no sense of self. Chaotic-enmeshed children have consistently been given excuses for failure to cope with life's obstacles or have not

Figure 5.1. Universe of Parent and Child Behavior.

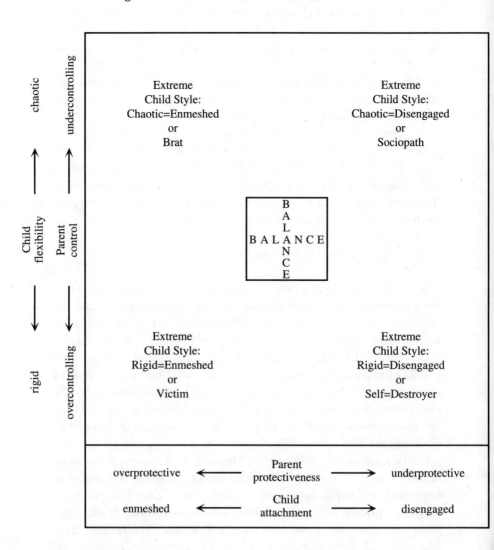

been even permitted to attempt to cope. For example, a chaotic-enmeshed child who attempts to climb a tree may be asked to sit next to his mother so he doesn't get hurt. The mother may successfully transfer her own fears to her child and convey the notion that being close to Mommy is more important than being independent. Chaotic-enmeshed children tend to be obnoxious as babies and become more and more unmanageable and disobedient as they grow up until their parents or other adults protect them less and control them more.

The Overprotective, Overcontrolling Parent

The overprotective, overcontrolling parent will attempt to buffer the child from any hurt, but, in addition, this parent will attempt to limit a child's freedom excessively. Often this parent has a perfectionistic style of behavior and may be vicariously seeking acclaim through the achievements of the child. The overprotective, overcontrolling parenting style will tend to produce a child who is very "good," but who is also rigid and enmeshed. In addition to taking on the characteristics of enmeshment as described in the preceding section, the child becomes *rigid,* that is, afraid to experiment, invent, modify, or even think. For example, when a rigid-enmeshed child begins to decorate a bike, a parent may criticize the child for attempting to improve upon the manufacturer. When a child is continually criticized or second-guessed, especially in conjunction with being overprotected, he or she will tend to shut down imaginative and creative processes in favor of following standardized, rigid prescriptions for behavior. Such children are compliant, but they doubt themselves and are afraid to take risks. The problem with this form of "good" behavior is that it usually entails children ignoring their own needs and putting their parents' needs first. These children tend to develop stomachaches, headaches, and other psychosomatic symptoms, as well as significant insecurity in peer relationships. The remedy is for the parent to loosen up on control and focus more on the child's needs.

The Underprotective, Undercontrolling Parent

The underprotective, undercontrolling parent will let the child "get away with murder," and because the child feels unloved and unprotected, he or she may eventually commit murder. Such children respect no authority and have little concern for anyone but themselves. A child who is chaotic and disengaged will need increased protection and increased control in order to recover.

The Underprotective, Overcontrolling Parent

The underprotective, overcontrolling parent is again perfectionist, but is so selfishly preoccupied that the child's nurturance is overlooked. As a result of adult overcontrol the child takes on rigid characteristics discussed in the preceding section. Children who are also underprotected become *disengaged,* withdrawing from caretakers who fail to protect them from hurtful or dangerous elements in their physical or social environment. One of these dangers is the caretaker's behavior, which may be neglectful or abusive. Underprotected children may fall out of windows or into swimming pools, or they may be yelled at, threatened, or hit by adults. The disengaged child develops self-destructive characteristics that parallel the destructive behavior of underprotective adults. These children do not feel loved, and may not be, and experience the world as a very lonely and fault-finding place. They may seem to comply with their parents' wishes but oppose them in a passive-aggressive way out of fear of censure. They tend to forget things, procrastinate, and have "accidents," for example, with cars. Another variant of this child pattern is more active and direct aggression and oppositionality. The rigid-disengaged child needs additional protection and less control in order to abandon defensiveness and self-destructiveness.

Balance and Child Self-Motivation

There is no question that children need control and protection. With control and protection children can develop the motivation to succeed and to acquire the other important values of our culture, such as loving, playing, and staying healthy. In a balanced environment, parental control and protection become intertwined with child flexibility and attachment; motivation proceeds, eventually, from internalized self-protection and self-control.

At early ages children are not capable of caring for themselves. When this insight prevails, parents watch or supervise young children at all times. When this insight fails, young children fall down wells, shoot themselves with handguns, or drown in swimming pools. But we cannot always watch children. What happens when the external agent is not around? Someday they will have to watch themselves. If our approaches to parenting protection and control are unbalanced, we will surely delay, sabotage, and even destroy the ability of children to watch themselves, that is, we will undermine their self-motivation.

Parenting by Automatic Pilot

There is a corollary to the principle of balanced protection and control: let children control "elective" life issues, and exert parental control only on the "essential" ones. Parents and others can decide what is essential and elective in child behavior. In an "automatic pilot" or "cruise control" state, children are left to make decisions as much as possible on their own, and parents retain veto power for use only in "essential," as opposed to "elective," areas of the child's life. Essential areas of child behavior include matters of health, safety, productivity, respect, and communication. Elective areas involve friends, hair, room decor, when and where to do homework, and, to some extent, bedtime. Figure 5.2 gives an approximation of the relative proportions of these two areas. Parents who focus on essential areas of child behavior will tend to not interfere in elective areas, and will leave as much decision making to children as they can handle. Children as young as three, with a little help from parents, can make very good decisions in most areas of life, essential as well as elective.

Systemic Assessment

Training caretakers of children in systems thinking is even more difficult than training them in dyadic assessment. The more forces that impinge upon and influence a child's behavior, the more difficult it is to understand. In systems assessment, the caretaker has to learn that the child's behavior is not primarily influenced by something inside the child or by something the parent or teacher is doing in and of itself, but by a number of different interacting

Figure 5.2. Child Behavior Locus of Control and Protection.

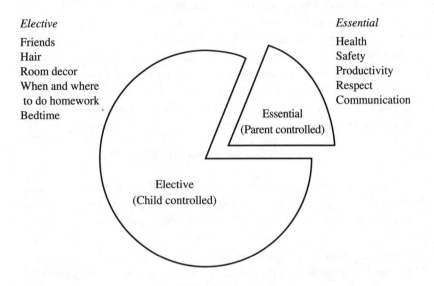

Elective

Friends
Hair
Room decor
When and where
  to do homework
Bedtime

Essential

Health
Safety
Productivity
Respect
Communication

Essential
(Parent controlled)

Elective
(Child controlled)

forces, such as conflicting expectations from a mother and father or from a parent and teacher. These conflicting messages put the child in the middle, between two adults, or at one point of a triangle through which adults detour their own communication and conflicts (Bowen, 1978; Minuchin, 1974). Many triangles are possible in the family and school subsystems and in the family-school "mesosystem" (Bronfenbrenner, 1979). Triangles can even occur with ideas, for example, when a mother is fighting against the memories of her own abused childhood by "underabusing," that is, overprotecting, her child. Triangulating behavior often stems from the adults' unresolved individual issues, but, in any case, it is a sign of unresolved conflict in their relationship. Child behavior that is enmeshed in overt and covert triangles is more difficult to understand, and individual and dyadic procedures will not work. The child problem needs to be understood as a mirror of, or metaphor for, the adult problems, and the assessment lens needs to focus on the adults' interactions with each other.

    Although it is not traditional for the school to take responsibility for the resolution of personal adult problems and dysfunctional family, school, and family-school triangles, child problems are not going to be prevented or solved until the school assumes this role. School personnel who are trained in systems and ecosystems assessment can see the big picture in which the child problem is embedded and thereby become empowered to solve problems that they otherwise could not. This is a kind of "second order" assessment in which school personnel begin to look at child behavior in a new way (Watzlawich, Weakland, and Fisch, 1974). A child behavior once labeled oppositional or stubborn, for example, can be seen as a normal coping device of someone pulled in two directions. Teachers can pass on their ecosystemic thinking to parents in formal and informal ways—by raising the issues of triangles in parent-teacher conferences, for example. Parents can also be trained directly by the ecosystems consultant, the school coordinator, or another person designated by the school. Ecosystems education or training is, of course, a major ingredient of collaborative team interventions. There are many ways for school staff, parents, and other collaborators to absorb ecosystems thinking. The most important requirement is that schools accept responsibility to do the job.

Summary

This chapter presents the argument that most mysterious, chronic, and severe child home and school behavioral and emotional problems are most likely motivational—not neurological, medical, or developmental—in nature. Motivational disorders are caused primarily by dysfunctions in adult, principally parent, management of children—specifically in the protection and control of children. Such dysfunctions derive from the parenting these adult managers received when they were children. For parents and other adult managers of children to raise healthy, happy, responsible, and successful children, they have to find the right balance in the use of protection and control. When adult problems interfere with effective parenting and education of children, the adults need to work on their own issues and get the children out of the middle. Systems therapists and ecosystems consultants can help parents and teachers distinguish their own issues from child problems and also gain perspective on how their behaviors influence the children in their care. Chapter Six presents specific strategies for solving child problems of an individual, dyadic, or systemic variety.

6

TRAINING FOR SYSTEMS INTERVENTIONS

The process of training collaborators, mainly parents and teachers, in how to raise and educate children and in how to solve child problems utilizes the same three levels—individual, dyadic, and systemic—that were presented in Chapter Five. Three brief case studies follow that illustrate the kinds of school-based situations for which ecosystemic collaborative intervention is required. These examples demonstrate how intrapsychic thinking, dysfunctional triangles, and parent/teacher/caretaker misuse of protection and control sap children of the motivational energy necessary to behave themselves and to achieve.

The "Special" and "Sensitive" Boy

Description of Problem

Gary, a seven-year-old boy, had had several ear operations and had lived virtually his whole life with tubes in his ears. More operations were being planned. In addition, Gary had been diagnosed as dyslexic and learning disabled, and was being "specially" educated, that is, given speech and language therapy in a structured classroom, and other "special" services. His parents had taken Gary to several "special"-ists and had been advised by all, as well as by their pediatrician, that Gary was a "special" and "sensitive" child and that because of his difficult life, they should, in effect, go easy on him and give him "special" treatment. Gary had a sister who was eleven, who was not specially treated, and who was doing fine, although this child's normal developmental issues of separation and individuation were not being dealt with properly because of the overfocus on Gary.

Gary was specially treated and was disruptive, distractible, underachieving, impolite at times, and generally difficult to manage, mostly at home. The parents had been advised by all the experts that because of Gary's many physical, neurological, and learning problems, they should expect a lifetime of behavioral problems with Gary. They were advised to be patient with the cross they had to bear.

Etiology and Maintenance of Problem

As is fairly clear in the description above, the problem with Gary was not in Gary, but in the thinking of the adults in his life. The behavioral problems that Gary exhibited were attributed to Gary's physical and learning problems and were excused as necessary concomitants of those problems. Gary was seen as a helpless victim of those problems and as having a diminished ability to behave himself or do his work as well as the other child in the family. The diagnosis for Gary's behavior problems was confused with his other diagnoses, and the result was a treatment plan that was incorrect and ineffective, that is, for his parents to be patient. The correct diagnosis for Gary's behavior problems is motivation deficit disorder, that is, a lack of motivation to behave, which is easily treatable through parental request, instruction, and, if necessary, enforcement.

In the case of Gary, a switch from parental intrapsychic thinking (the problem is in Gary) to interactional thinking (the problem is in the adult caretaking style) would have prevented the development of Gary's behavioral and underachievement problems—or solved them once they started. In addition to bad advice from "experts" and "special"-ists, Gary's mother and father disagreed on how much to expect of their son. This is a common characteristic of parents with "problem" children. In this case, the father was more sympathetic to Gary because, as a male and as the youngest child, the boy reminded him of his own need to be protected from the harsh realities of the world. (His wife provided this protection.)

"Sweetheart"

Description of Problem

Jacqui, a fifteen-year-old girl, had been force-fed for her first six years because of a medical problem and then given special treatment all her life. Jacqui had been given every possible educational and psychological test and service at school and every possible concession at home to make life easier for her. Her older brother had shown signs of underachievement and learning disability, but more was expected of him, and he was currently doing fine as a junior in high school. Jacqui had a younger brother who was also doing fine. Despite thousands of hours of special treatment over fifteen years, Jacqui was failing tenth grade and doing worse than ever. While Jacqui's father babied her and called her "Sweetheart," he also secretly resented her need for special treatment. He periodically insulted her and at times would explode in frustration and hit her. On one occasion he attempted to choke her and Jacqui called the Department of Child and Youth Services to report him for child abuse. Mom and Dad, as usual, disagreed on how tough to be on Jacqui. The parents' marriage was of questionable vitality. No interaction was noted between husband and wife during several interview sessions.

Etiology and Maintenance of Problem

Jacqui's problem stemmed largely from the thinking and behavior of the adults in her life. Jacqui was given excuses for her behavior, which was attributed to medical causes. The adults conspired, unconsciously or consciously, to avoid correct diagnosis because of personal, marital, or family-school conflicts. The deception was most costly to Jacqui, who should have been diagnosed with MDD.

Metaphorical Rebellion

Description of Problem

A fourteen-year-old ninth-grade boy, Carl, acted out at home and was barely passing at school. He was also abusing drugs, and had recently impregnated a girl. The mother and father habitually disagreed on the correct response to Carl's behavior. The father tended to be strict and even brutal at times, while the mother protected Carl from his father. The father treated the mother much the same way he treated Carl, and she used tactics similar to Carl's to strike back. She couldn't fight back directly, so she used indirect methods—withdrawal of affection and sex and fighting over the treatment of Carl. Carl, meanwhile, felt supported by his mother and continued his indirect fight with his father through underachievement and other passive-aggressive strategies. Carl's sister, eleven years old, was also showing symptoms of behavior disorder and underachievement.

Etiology and Maintenance of Problem

Again, with this family, we see the familiar pattern: parental disagreement on parenting and marital problems. School efforts to solve Carl's problems had been ineffective. At age fifteen, Carl dropped out of school, left home, and moved in with a friend. His mother had recently discovered that her husband had been conducting an affair out of town over the past six months.

Individual Intervention

If a child is found to be hungry, he obviously needs some food. If he can't see well, glasses will probably help. If he can't write, then he needs to be helped to write. In my experience, child problems that are truly individually based are usually solved fairly easily.

Even problems that are primarily neurological usually have clear solutions, although they may not be totally satisfying because of the physical limitations involved.

Dyadic Intervention

When the primary problem is centered in a relationship problem between two people—a parent and a child or a teacher and a child, without significant triangulating among the adults and children— the problem is called dyadic. In dyadic relationships, a "linear" problem is solved by one or both parties simply doing more or less of a problematic behavior, for example, a parent lecturing less or a child complying more. L'Abate, Baggett, and Anderson (1984) support the notion of linear intervention for linear problems. These authors suggest that "most problems that appear in the practice of clinical child psychology and family therapy are straightforward and should be treated that way" (p. 16). Linear treatment is the kind of prescription that might be given by Dinkmeyer and McKay (1976), Ginott (1965, 1969), Dreikurs and Soltz (1964), Gordon (1980), and other parent educators, or in the behavior parent training literature, for example, Patterson and Brodsky (1966) or Atkenson and Forehand (1978). The dyadic directives provided in this chapter follow the schema in the dyadic assessment section in Chapter Five and are divided into procedures for four types, paralleling the parenting dysfunctions outlined there.

This section describes methods of successful intervention for parents who are overcontrolling, undercontrolling, overprotecting, or underprotecting their children or who are using some combination of these dysfunctional approaches. Changes in parent behavior are the main influence on concomitant changes in child dysfunctional behavior. Four sections of methods will be offered, corresponding to the four quadrants of parent-child behavior shown in Figure 5.1. Modifications will be needed for parents who do not fit any of the "classic" patterns, for example, parents who are undercontrolling, but not overprotective. Although training and advice in this section are addressed primarily to parents, teachers and other child caretakers can profit from it as well.

The Overcontrolling, Overprotecting Parent:
Finding a Way to Say Yes

There are few more discouraging and upsetting experiences for a child than to be ignored, contradicted, lectured, and told no by parents, in short, to be overcontrolled and overprotected. This is especially true when, as is often the case, the child has intelligently considered alternative plans of action and made what he or she thinks are good decisions. When parents overcontrol and overprotect, the result is a child who thinks of him- or herself as incapable, incompetent, and unable to deal with the tasks facing him. This child is considered by others as a professional victim.

"Parenting by questions" is a technique I developed to help parents avoid the extremes of protection and control. Questioning is a powerful technique because it asks the other party to say something back, to reveal something about him- or herself, or to reveal a thought or an attitude. Parenting by questions is recommended for parents who are overcontrolling and/or overprotecting because it involves asking questions instead of giving answers, warnings, threats, punishments, or other adult directives. This strategy indirectly shifts the focus of responsibility onto the child, asking him or her to give an opinion, consider alternatives, make a plan, reassure the parent, or perhaps suggest consequences if promised activities or agreements are not carried out. Parenting by questions targets essential areas of child behavior, such as health and safety, and leaves elective areas, such as hairstyle and homework schedule, up to the children. It results in automatic pilot, self-regulated, or cruise control behavior on the part of the children.

There are many advantages to using questions to guide children:

1. It provides access to the child's thoughts. This access may be the main protection against all dangers to children. If we know what children are thinking, we can help them to avoid mistakes and take good care of themselves.
2. It allows parents to avoid giving instructions or lectures about things that the child already knows.
3. It gives children a chance to make decisions and plans for them-

selves. Further, children can get feedback on their plans and a chance to enhance their self-esteem through making decisions that work. Parents are already supposed to know how to do these things.

4.   It avoids fights. If children can show that they have made a good plan for themselves, then parents don't have to say no so much. No, as we know, is close to the worst thing you can say to a child.

5.   It conserves energy. When parents ask questions and children answer, the children do most of the work.

Teenage Freedom: Parenting by Questions

The following example of parenting by questions is presented in an attempt to make the procedure more understandable. Two scenarios are given; the first is less preferred and the second is more preferred. In this example, a mother and her teenage son discuss his desire to go out.

Parent-Teenager Interaction: Scenario A

Child (age sixteen):   Mom, can I go out tonight?

Mom: Where?

Child: John's.

Mom: Why?

Child: He's having a few friends over.

Mom: Who are they?

Child: Phil, Amy, Todd, and some others.

Mom: Are they drug addicts?

Child: No!

Mom: Are the parents home?

Child: I'm not sure.

Mom: Well, find out.

Child: And I want to stay out 'til one o'clock.

Mom: That's out of the question. Midnight is already too late.

Child: Mom, I'm sixteen, and I've always been responsible.

Mom: Just the same, kids are into all kinds of things these days, and my job is to protect you.

Child: I'm getting sick of this. Don't you trust me?

Mom: I trust you. It's those others I don't trust.

Child: How about twelve thirty?

Mom: Nope. Twelve midnight. That's my final decision.

The preceding is a very brief example of the oppositional, adversarial interaction in which many parents and children become engaged. It leaves both parties feeling guilty, angry, frustrated, and otherwise upset. The child often pushes the limit. The parent then overlooks the violation or punishes it, in either case making things even worse. Consider the alternative approach outlined in Scenario B.

Parent-Teenager Interaction: Scenario B

Child (age 16): Mom, I want to go out tonight.

Mom: OK. Where are you going?

Child: To John's.

Mom: Are you going to be safe?

Child: (good naturedly) No, I'm going to get arrested.

Mom: Just checking. When will you be home?

Child: Oh, about one.

Mom: Are you sure you want to stay out that late?

Child: Well, I might be home earlier. I just want the flexibility, and I don't want you to worry.

Mom: O.K. Leave me a number where you can be reached and call
if you need anything.

Child: OK. Thanks, Mom.

After the conversation in Scenario B, the speakers feel good
about each other, trust and appreciation have been reinforced, and
the child has had a chance to problem solve, reassure his parent, and
make commitments. This approach works just as well for children
of all ages and for many types of problem situations.

What If Something Goes Wrong?

Parents frequently ask, "What if something goes wrong?" The
answer: Much is already going wrong, with epidemic statistics on
disobedience, lying, running away, drinking, deceptive scams, vio-
lence, suicide, and manslaughter through car accidents and fights.
If something goes wrong in Scenario B, it will probably be less
disastrous than the result of Scenario A, and it should lead to another
round of parenting by questions. I have found this method to be very
effective. Many authoritarian methods—hollering, giving lectures,
and grounding youngsters—are often clearly unnecessary, which
renders them ineffective. Parenting by questions greatly accelerates
the assumption of responsibility by children, gets them into automatic pilot or cruise control, and results in warm, low-problem,
delightful relationships between parents and children.

The Undercontrolling, Overprotective Parent:
Victory Strategies for Parent Hostages

Constructive, direct methods, such as establishing firm rules and
consequences for persistent misbehavior, are necessary when children are unwilling to negotiate with parents. Effective parenting
includes the ability to say no. This section will focus on how parents overprotect and undercontrol, and how children become
"brats" or "child terrorists" in response. Case examples will be
provided and strategies will be described that will enable parents to
control their children without resorting to incorrect "neuroedumed-

ical" diagnoses or abusive, overcorrective measures like lecturing, threatening, grounding, and hitting. In situations like these, strategies and tactics are truly necessary, since at this stage children are really acting like an enemy.

"Brats" or "child terrorists" are children who not only want to do things their own way, which is fairly normal, but who expect to get their own way all the time, and who oppose all obstacles that stand in their way. Often these chaotic children have had some medical, nutritional, developmental, or situational problem in early childhood and their parents understandably feel sorry for them. These children may have had hearing problems, tubes implanted in their ears, or difficulty swallowing or digesting food. They may have been emotionally neglected during a bitter divorce. Whatever the source of the early difficulty, when parents feel too sorry for their children or treat them too "specially," the children are likely to imagine additional handicaps and expect special treatment, whether or not it is related to a legitimate difficulty. These "sensitive," "allergic," or "hyperactive," children are not expected to handle the normal tasks and stresses of everyday life.

When a child is treated as "special" for a sufficient period of time, he or she begins to internalize this concept and to act accordingly, with or without justification. When parents and other adult figures begin to feel abused by the child's demands, their attempts to defend themselves and request more reasonable child behavior are met with defiance. As President Nixon demonstrated during the Watergate Affair in 1973, once people experience being powerful, they are very reluctant to give it up—and children are as susceptible as adults. Parents who feel alternately furious and sympathetic, and generally guilty, are no match for adversaries such as these.

Rethinking the Handicap

Probably the most important step in learning to control coercive children is to change the way we think about them. Parents of these children have often been so indoctrinated in what children can't do that they expect less of children and, not surprisingly, get less. A shift needs to be made from negative thinking, that is, from a focus on what our children can't do, to positive thinking, that is, to a focus on what they can do. Rosenthal (1966) showed that teachers given high and low expectations of children actually taught them in such different ways that the children's standardized test scores shifted significantly by the end of the year to accord with those expectations. Similarly, no matter what a child's physical, mental, or emotional handicap may be, if the adult's vision is positive, the child will be helped to visualize successful outcomes for him- or herself. The motivational research literature has shown dramatically that the most successful athletes and other professionals are those that write down goals and action plans, talk to themselves positively, and vividly imagine the success they will achieve (Meyer, 1984.)

As well as learning to emphasize the positive, parents must be helped to examine the specific handicaps or problems their children are supposed to have. A careful review of virtually every handicap can result in the conclusion that there is no necessary connection between the handicap and coercive activity. All children who have difficulty can learn to ask for help and can control emotional outbursts when they are frustrated. Children know this. It is their parents who need to change their thinking and become less sympathetic and more truly helpful.

Strategies for Coping with Child Terrorists

As was mentioned earlier in this chapter, the first and best strategy for dealing with children is to do it their way. Through parenting by questions, children can be given practice in decision-making and can build their self-esteem. But when children are not willing to be reasonable or negotiate, then a line must be drawn. Parents must be willing to use "veto power" when necessary.

The following set of procedures for parents has been found to be extremely effective in helping children to comply with reasonable parental expectations and to desist from terrorist or insurgent activity:

1. Secure agreement from your spouse or any other significant parenting figure regarding the need for change in the behavior of one or more of the children. This may very well be the most

difficult step in the process. Without this step, further progress will be difficult or impossible.

2. Call a meeting of the entire family to express the opinion that you, the parent, are feeling abused, and that you need things to change. Tell everyone that you would like their cooperation in negotiating some new rules and procedures. This usually catches everyone's attention and sometimes leads directly to the setting of new family rules.

3. If one or more members of the family are unwilling to cooperate at this stage, tell them that you are prepared to take matters into your own hands. This step assumes that you, the parent, have really come to terms with how desperate the situation is and are prepared to do whatever it takes, even to separate from your spouse, to get matters under control.

4. If both parents are united in their resolve to help their coercive child or children to change, and the children are willing, begin to negotiate. Parenting by questions will be helpful here. As much as possible, the plan should come from the children. Children are often much more capable than we think. Suggestions can be made by parents, but they should, as much as possible, be ratified by the children.

5. Secure agreement by all parties to the new set of rules, and identify consequences for failure to follow the rules. Time on a child's bed, with "no toys and no noise," and with the door open, is a most effective consequence for misbehavior or failure to comply.

6. When children are not willing to lie on their bed, parents are advised to lay their children on their backs on the floor, hold their wrists down, and sit gently but firmly on their thighs for whatever time is necessary to gain compliance. This activity has been called "exorcism" by a few parents and is really the least abusive or damaging method of all those used by parents on terrorist children. The exorcism takes anywhere from zero seconds, when the mere mention of this method is enough to gain child compliance, to two or three hours, on some occasions. Parents who are in agreement about parenting rarely have to use this method more than two or three times. Parents not in agreement about parenting, as mentioned before, are unlikely to find anything that works. Separation and divorce will usually help severely conflicting parents but, even

when this occurs, disagreements often continue to wreak havoc upon children's attitudes and behavior after the divorce. Children held on the floor should be let up if, and only if, they agree to lie on their bed as requested or for periodic necessities, such as eating or going to the bathroom. Time spent on the floor should be added to time on the bed, since the children have bothered parents that much more than with the original offense. This time on the bed has been called "time out (from positive reinforcement)" in the professional literature, and, more informally, "doing time," "getting minutes," or "groundation" by some child clients. Children should only be let off their beds after agreeing to behave themselves.

7.   When children come out of their rooms, they should be granted all the privileges and rights of a family citizen with no further repercussions or revenge. Further misbehavior should be dealt with in the same manner as described above, with additional time periods assessed.

8.   In noncrisis conversations, parents and children can discuss how they're doing and any changes in the family rules that might be helpful. After a crisis occurs, parents and children should go back to loving and having fun together. Parents should hug their children, touch them, and frequently ask them how they are doing. Love and communication are the best defenses against all child problems.

Using Caution

The procedures described in this section, while very effective in solving child terrorist disorder (CTD), are sometimes difficult to implement consistently and confidently. Parents who were raised by abusive parents or who were spoiled as children may find it difficult to follow these guidelines; they will do well to work with a therapist. Parents may also have been influenced by various professional "experts" who have convinced them of their child's "handicap" and need for special treatment and, because of these factors, may have misgivings about these procedures. It is hoped that the methods suggested here will be perceived as humane, effective, and good for children, who will quickly resume being responsible, successful, and happy—a behavioral and emotional pattern most predictive of the development of high self-esteem in children.

The Overcontrolling, Underprotective Parent: Parenting Without Anger

There are two varieties of underprotected children—the overcontrolled and undercontrolled. Aggressive or passive-aggressive behavior is adopted by children when one or more parent is overcontrolling and underprotective. This behavior is essentially oppositional, but it is sometimes presented as compliance, so that it is not active and overt opposition, but indirect and passive. The overcontrolling, underprotective parent is usually the father, but sometimes it is the mother. In any case, the other parent, when there is one, usually takes an opposite overprotective, undercontrolling position, and the parents fight indirectly through the children. Children who are passive-aggressive are usually very angry, but because they fear the overcontrolling parent, they become depressed, and express their anger indirectly through accidents, forgetting, and underachievement. The parent involved in situations like these is very confused and angry and gets locked in a vicious circle with the child: neither will change until the other does.

The solution to active- or passive-aggressive behavior in children is the movement of the dysfunctional parent behavior toward less control and more protection. For this to happen, this parent must be willing to give up control and anger and realize that the child is malfunctioning mainly in response to the parent's dysfunction. As the dysfunctional parent makes changes, the spouse and child will make complementary changes. To accomplish this goal, it is helpful for the child to speak more directly about his or her anger and for the parent and child to negotiate a fairer deal regarding the use of freedom, for example, through parenting by questions. As the cause of the child's dysfunction (that is, anger at his or her parent) becomes clear, the parent can agree to offer the child as much freedom as the child can handle. The child will usually appreciate this, use the freedom responsibly, and take greater risks in speaking directly to the parent.

The Undercontrolling/Underprotective
Parent: Learning to Care

When parents are undercontrolling and underprotective, it is possible that no amount of help or advice will change them. These are people who are probably the victims of child abuse and neglect themselves and know no other way to live or parent. They may have developed a chronic and severe pattern of selfishness, addiction, and irresponsibility, and may be incapable of change. The children of these parents are the ones most likely to steal, cheat, abuse drugs and alcohol, drop out of school, vandalize, hurt others, and even kill.

The solution to a situation involving parents who are underprotective and undercontrolling may ultimately be the removal of the child from the home. Extensive effort should, of course, first be made to talk to the parent in an empathetic and nurturing fashion, and to assist the parent with problems of economic survival or drug addiction. These efforts may or may not be successful, however, and when they are not, the help of other family members or the Department of Child and Youth Services may be necessary to arrange alternative residence for the children involved. Children in these situations will behave very chaotically and usually will oppose efforts to control them.

Systemic Intervention

A third level of intervention is based on more systemic considerations. In these situations children's problems are not primarily individual or reflective of dyadic relationship dysfunctions. Rather, they derive from adult individual or relationship problems into which children are drawn and triangulated. The most common kind of triangle is the one in which mother and father are in conflict and fight their battle by arguing over parenting, thereby confusing the child, creating a hierarchy vacuum, and placing the child in the bind of having to choose between the parents. Other triangles can develop at home, at school, between home and school, and between various agencies. Many writers have offered suggestions on dealing with systems triangles (Bowen, 1978; Foster, 1984; Haley, 1987; Minuchin, 1974; Power and Bartholomew 1987).

Training is the principal vehicle for systems intervention within the school-based ecosystemic collaboration model: all school personnel need to be trained in ecosystems thinking and empowered to use this knowledge in their interactions with parents, other school staff, and community players. This process will become a contagious and reverberating one which will have greater effects than a limited number of collaborative team interventions conducted by the ecosystems consultant. The ultimate goal of the collaborative model is for each person in charge of children to assume a high level of responsibility for child success.

Systems intervention within a school-based program involve more than anything else a willingness to be honest about what you think and what you perceive. Intervention training for school personnel can certainly include instruction in the use of reframing, restraining, utilization, and other family therapy techniques, but in my experience what is usually most needed is good communication skills. Carkhuff's (1969) list of these skills, mentioned in Chapter Four, is a good one: empathy, warmth, respect, concreteness, genuineness, self-disclosure, confrontation, and immediacy. The enablement and empowerment principles described by Dunst and Trivette (1987), for example, allowing help to be reciprocated, are also at times very important. Armed with ecosystemic awareness, communication skills, and principles of empowerment, school personnel can get their own house (namely, their school) in better shape, look in the mirror at their own personal lives, and establish closer and more honest relationships with parents and other child caretakers. A particular person may seem at times impossible to deal with from the point of view of one collaborator or another—parent, teacher, principal, or other party. It is the job of the ecosystems consultant to help the school avoid adversarial relationships and to help resolve them when they occur.

Summary

The strategies presented in this chapter for changing dysfunctional styles of parenting and child management are based on my belief and opinion that child behavior will change—most reliably and dramatically—in response to changes in the behavior of parents and other significant adults.

Saying yes is a most powerful tool for raising happy and successful children. Parenting by questions and giving children choices are often very effective methods for helping childen, no matter what problems they have, to practice decision-making, interpersonal skills, and general competency. Parents using these methods will have to say no to their children less frequently.

When parents, in their desire to care for their children, overprotect and undercontrol them, the reasons may be in family-of-origin experiences, guilt about long working hours away from the children, or some handicap or difficulty the child may have or be thought to have. The child's response may be to grasp and wield the proffered power imperiously. Although parents must listen to the advice of many "experts," they should seriously consider taking a harder line if their child becomes coercive and demanding. Various methods are effective, including negotiation, democratic rule-setting, securing agreements, and providing consequences for noncompliance. For counter-insurgence tactics to be effective, parental agreement is essential, and assistance from an ecosystemic consultant is often helpful, or even necessary.

The solutions to the underprotective parenting dysfunctions are usually more complicated and difficult. Underprotective parents are often entrenched in their behavior patterns and are themselves real victims of much abuse.

A clear understanding of exactly what advice—linear or ecosystemic—to give to parents, teachers, and other child managers for the correction of a wide variety of child misbehavior is essential to the effective functioning of a school-based ecosystemic collaboration program.

Within a collaborative format, the goal is for collaborators to learn about boundaries, alliances, coalitions, family and school structures, triangles, and other systemic and ecosystemic concepts and to work on their own problems individually or in groups. When the problem goes beyond the child, the implicated adults have to be willing to see and accept the message the child is giving through the problematic behavior pattern. Individual therapy, marital therapy, family-school collaboration and encouragement, and support by third parties are all ways to solve or ameliorate problems in a larger system.

Part Three

COLLABORATIVE
TEAM
INTERVENTIONS

7

CHILDREN MISDIAGNOSED
WITH
INTRAPSYCHIC PROBLEMS

The labeling of children with intrapsychic diagnoses and the application of standard concomitant treatments are among the most destructive processes in American society today. Each of the following cases involves a child who has been given an intrapsychic label but whose major problem is primarily motivational deficit disorder stemming from adult training deficit disorders. By labeling these children incorrectly with neurological, developmental, psychiatric, or other intrapsychic disabilities that are either nonexistent or secondary to the primary problem, adult professionals postpone and retard real solutions to children's problems, which need to come from changes in relationships among adults and between adults and children.

I Can See the Ball Again

Background

Jeremy, a ten-year-old boy in the fourth grade, had been diagnosed at age six as learning disabled and suffering from attention deficit hyperactivity disorder (ADHD), and he had already been retained once. As a labeled special education child, he had spent part of every day of his first four school years in the elementary school learning center. In addition, he had been given a mild dose of Ritalin (7.5 milligrams daily) for four years on the advice of a pediatric neurologist whom the parents and school personnel considered an "expert." Jeremy had also been provided with summer tutoring by the learning center teacher, individual in-school counseling by the school psychologist, and language therapy by the speech therapist who, in addition to language work, initiated a behavior modification program for his poor social behavior. The learning center teacher had had literally hundreds of consultations with the mother over the years, and the mother had seen two or three psychiatrists, who had all prescribed antidepressant medications for her. While the idea of marriage counseling had been discussed in the mother's therapy, few marital sessions had taken place, reportedly because her husband was resistive. After all these attempts at helping young Jeremy over four years, in literally thousands of hours of formal and informal efforts by home and school, Jeremy was unimproved and perhaps worse. At the beginning of his fifth year at the elementary school the school decided to refer Jeremy and his family to the family-school collaboration program.

What follows is a list of school complaints, or "presenting concerns," regarding Jeremy that appeared on the referral form used by the collaboration program:

- Poor social behavior.
- Difficulty maintaining friendships.
- Negativistic and antagonistic attitude toward peers (long-standing problem since grade 1).
- Resistant to school work.
- Easily frustrated.
- Distractible.
- Produces minimal work in learning center.
- Appears angry with teachers.
- Talks, shouts back.
- Makes statements like "You don't have time for me" and "You didn't teach me that yet."

- Apathetic.
- Low self-esteem.
- Desires to spend more time in regular grade 5 classroom.
- Dislikes language therapy.

Assessment and Intervention

Because of the many previous efforts with Jeremy, the case was referred immediately for collaborative team intervention. The first collaborative team meeting with Jeremy and his family was attended by ten people: Jeremy, his father and mother, his regular teacher, his learning center teacher, his language teacher, the school psychologist (who set up the meeting), the school nurse, the school principal, and the ecosystems consultant. Jeremy's tenth-grade sister was out of town and could not attend the session. The meeting began with everyone describing the problem, which was stated in much the same terms as were listed on the referral form. There were several differences, however, from previous intervention formats:

1. Jeremy was present to hear everyone discussing him together. This format conveys respect for the child's ability to handle information about himself that is sometimes withheld from so-called handicapped children.

2. Jeremy was asked his opinion and invited to interact with staff members and parents regarding diagnosis and solution. This conveyed an expectation of involvement and an attitude of respect to him.

3. The open forum allowed everyone to hear all opinions and permitted all present to interact. In this collaborative environment, new and different information about Jeremy had a greater chance of being noticed than it would in one-to-one or smaller group interactions. Also, information that might have been given only to some could become public knowledge, for everyone to hear. By virtue of the number and importance of the people present, and the sad story of adult ineffectiveness and student failure that emerged, a strong need developed to solve the problem fast. It was possible for individuals to deny the problem one at a time, to get discouraged, and procrastinate;

but with everyone present, extra pressure was generated on participants to finally help the child. If nothing else, failure was embarrassing.

4. Through the introduction of a competent ecosystems consultant, group interactions were skillfully orchestrated, and new ideas and methods were introduced.

The following actions were taken during the collaborative team intervention with Jeremy:

1. The use of Ritalin was discontinued.
2. Jeremy was allowed to earn more time in the regular classroom.
3. Jeremy was defined as "unhandicapped" and "just as good as his smart sister." This redefinition was crucial not only for Jeremy but for everyone else present.
4. Jeremy was asked to help develop and approve the plan for his success.
5. Jeremy was asked to stop his temper tantrums immediately, conveying a belief in his ability to control himself. Unpleasant consequences were prescribed if the tantrums continued, mainly having to spend "boring" time flat on his bed.
6. A "circle" meeting was arranged to discuss Jeremy's social problems and to find solutions to them. This meeting was held in Jeremy's mainstream classroom and was attended by Jeremy, his family, school staff, and Jeremy's regular classmates.
7. School staff continued to view the problem as motivational and focused on cooperating with Jeremy's parents to motivate Jeremy to do his work.

Results

In the case of Jeremy, the results were good. Jeremy did discontinue the use of Ritalin and felt much better. On the ball field, he said he could "see the ball again," and hit a grand-slam home run soon after stopping use of the medication. Jeremy's father, especially, was happy, since he never liked the idea, or the slightly immobilizing effect, of the medication. Jeremy's "circle" meeting was extremely successful, leading to better relations with his peers, more control for Jeremy, and new willingness to come to the teacher in case of conflict. Jeremy continued to have some problems staying on task, but there were signs of improvement, and because of his behavioral improvement, the school staff was more hopeful that academic progress would continue.

Jeremy's mother and father began marital therapy with the school consultant. The mother discontinued individual therapy with the psychiatrist, as well as the use of her antidepressant medication. The father gradually began to moderate his view that his wife was the main, or the only, problem, and to put more effort into pleasing her. The mother began to moderate her demandingness and to give her husband "the benefit of the doubt." The parents were both very happy with Jeremy's behavior, and the father began to help him every night with his reading. The school staff was extremely pleased with the intervention because for the first time in four years they felt in control of the problem and confident they were making progress.

Discussion

Reframing "neurological" child problems as motivational often helps to solve problems that are not primarily neurologically based. Most child problems are primarily of a motivational, not a biological or neurological, nature and are maintained by adult ignorance or dysfunctional relationships. In the case of Jeremy, reframing the problem as motivational allowed all those involved, including the child, to see the problem from a different perspective, which made it solvable. The school is an ideal site for the initiation and implementation of this reframing process. Jeremy's mother returned to therapy periodically to work on her self-esteem, and for six months for family therapy involving a niece whom she took in as a boarder. Jeremy's father joined a men's group. At last report, three years following the collaborative team intervention, Jeremy was very happy and successful, socially and academically.

I Don't Want to Be a Handicapped Child

Background

Marie was eleven and in sixth grade at the time of the first collaborative team intervention session. She had been underachieving, distractible, and a general pest for all of her elementary school career. Complaints about Marie went all the way back to her private preschool teacher. The sixth-grade teacher was regarded as an excellent motivator and had tried everything she knew to motivate Marie. In addition, she had called and met with Marie's parents on several occasions and had consulted with the school psychologist on the management of Marie.

Marie had one older sister, thirteen years old and in eighth grade, who was reported to be achieving and behaving appropriately. Marie's parents were both middleclass and high-achieving. They had been separated for one year, and were still actively in conflict over parenting and other issues. The consultant had heard through the grapevine prior to the first session that the father had questioned one of the town's school administrators about the advisability of participating in the collaboration program. The father had, in addition, called several acquaintances in an attempt to get more information about it. As is often the case with parents of problem children, there was substantial resistance to facing the problem, and months passed before the parents agreed to the meeting. The first session was held in the last quarter of the school year.

Assessment and Intervention

The first collaborative session was attended by the whole family, that is, the parents and their two children, and by the school psychologist, the sixth-grade teacher, the school principal, and the ecosystems consultant. The session began with the usual recounting by all present of the history of the problem and of individual perceptions and judgments regarding its cause and solution. The parents reported advice from various professionals and others attributing Marie's problems to laziness, hyperactivity, being "young for her age," and other causes. During this stage the disagreements among the session participants began to emerge. From the beginning of the session, the mother and father were observed to relate differently to Marie. Though they sat on either side of Marie in the circle, the father sat close to Marie and appeared to be protective of her, intercepting and interpreting remarks about her or to her. His arm was on the back of her chair. In response to direct questions, Marie talked in a somewhat disorganized fashion, in a voice like that of a child of perhaps five. She talked nervously and alternated between smiling and looking confused.

Sensing the familiar disagreements between parents about parenting and the overprotectiveness of the father, the consultant chose to attack the problem by provoking Marie. He asked her what she thought about the situation and how capable she thought she was. She replied that she thought she could do better, but that she was lazy and that the work was becoming more difficult. The consultant noted that she had been having problems since preschool. He asked her if she realized she was becoming a "handicapped" child and if she wanted to continue on the "road to being handicapped." At this point, the father angrily intervened and accused the consultant of cruel and unprofessional conduct. He increased his closeness to his daughter and she began to cry. The level of tension was great, and the father began to get up to leave. The consultant asked the father how frustrated he was with the problem and how much he wanted to solve it. The father agreed that things were serious and began to sit back down.

After everyone calmed down a bit, the consultant proceeded to give his analysis of the situation. He said he thought that Marie's problem was motivational, and that it was inadvertently, but primarily, caused by the parents' disagreements and the father's protectiveness of Marie against the expectations of the "cruel" school. He said the mother's and father's attitudes no doubt came from their upbringing and perhaps other factors. He said that the answer to the problem was for the parents to ask Marie to "shape up" and do her work, and to provide negative consequences, like time on the bed, if she didn't. He asked Marie whether she thought his ideas were fair. Marie said she agreed with the consultant and that his recommendations were fair.

After some additional processing, the consultant suggested a one- or two-week experiment during which Marie would take home a daily report card containing grades on specific behaviors expected of her in school, for example, paying attention and handing in homework. The grades were to result in home consequences, either positive (free time) or negative (time on the bed). Each of five grades was to have a one-hour consequence at home. All parties were advised to keep in touch with one another and to "sound the alarm" if the agreement was breaking down for any reason—for example, if the father was getting scared and was neglecting to impose consequences. Everyone agreed to the experiment, and a follow-up meeting was scheduled two weeks hence.

Results

The results of the one-session collaborative intervention with Marie were dramatic. Because Marie was upset at the meeting, her parents took her home from school after the meeting. On the way home, Marie told her parents that she didn't want to be "handicapped" anymore. The next day in school, the teacher observed her to be what he called "completely different." The teacher characterized her behavior as "a 180-degree turnaround." She was polite, age-appropriate, and productive. She was, in all respects, "a completely different child."

At the second, and last, collaboration meeting, the teacher reported the excellent results to the assembled group. The participants were the same. The "news" was not news to anyone except the consultant because everyone had been communicating with each other. The parents were delighted and reported significant changes in home behavior as well. Marie was more polite at home, more compliant, more cooperative with her siblings, and was even initiating work around the house. Marie's teacher asked Marie to explain her "turnaround," and she was extremely articulate. In the session as well, she was a completely different person. The change was truly inspiring. It was agreed by all that this would be our last session, but that we would keep in touch and reassemble if things began to deteriorate.

Discussion

Marie's underachievement, behavior problems, and general immaturity had been caused and maintained by her father's overprotectiveness and the marital problem. Shifting the diagnosis from intrapsychic causes, like hyperactivity, to interactional causes was crucial to the solution of the problem. The school-based ecosystemic collaborative format increased the clarity and intensity of the school personnel's feedback to the family and the likelihood that the parents would listen and act on the information. The ecosystems consultant provided the expertise in interactional diagnosis and the courage and skill to confront issues in a manner that was direct and forceful, though respectful. In two sessions of work, approximately four hours in duration, the consultant was able, with help from all collaborators involved, to lead the way in restructuring a situation into more positive and functional sequences and interactions. An additional benefit of the session was teacher training. As a result of one session of collaboration, Marie's teacher spontaneously took charge of conducting session two as if she were a veteran systems therapist. This she did well and with no formal training. A middle school follow-up with Marie and her family the following year revealed that Marie was still doing well.

$$6 \times 3 = 18$$

Background

Linda, seven, a second grader, had been experiencing mild difficulty in reading since first grade. She was achieving at an average level in other subjects. Tests by the reading specialist, school psychologist, pediatrician, and ophthalmologist showed no structural or ability problems. In addition, Linda read voluminously, fast, and with excellent comprehension at home. Linda's parents were high achievers themselves, very polite, and otherwise appropriate, and very concerned about their daughter's academic problems. Her father was an architect and her mother was a teacher. Linda had one older brother, a fifth grader, who was functioning well thus far. Linda had no behavior problems, and, though shy, did have friends. Linda wore glasses and was not as much of a "star" as her older brother.

The school's response to Linda's problem had been to assign her to special in-school tutoring twice a week with the reading specialist. This plan had been in operation for two years and was in place at the time of the first collaboration session with the ecosystems consultant, which took place toward the end of the school year. Linda's parents had been increasingly frustrated and had met with the school psychologist of the elementary school. The school psychologist had suggested many times to the parents that the "reading" problem was motivational, not neurological, physical, or educational, but the parents were not convinced.

Assessment and Intervention

After a second year of school meetings with Linda's parents, and after several months of parent resistance to meeting with the eco-systems consultant, the first collaborative team intervention was held. It was attended by the parents, their two children, the teacher, the school psychologist, the principal, and the reading specialist. Within minutes, the dynamics began to unfold. The teacher revealed that she was not overly concerned about Linda's performance, that it was after all average, and that Linda was experiencing some lesser difficulty with math, as well. The teacher thought that Linda's achievement was acceptable, and that she might achieve at higher levels later in life as a result of developmental changes. The mother presented as a somewhat nervous person, overly protective of her daughter. The father was less protective and concerned, it seemed, but still motivated to find a solution. Both parents revealed that they were high achievers in school and wanted Linda to be well prepared for college. They also were concerned about her general level of happiness and adjustment. The reading specialist spoke about and to Linda in a childlike voice, no doubt designed to help Linda feel more comfortable, but which, from the consultant's viewpoint, contributed to Linda's lack of motivation and responsibility through its "infantilizing" tone. This reading consultant, who was also trying to help Linda in other subjects, indicated that she was mystified and concerned that despite hours of training in the task of multiplying six times three, Linda could never remember that the correct answer is eighteen. The consultant began to get the picture that the extra time with the specialist was really, in all probability, reinforcing Linda's perceptions of herself as special, helpless, and incapable.

The psychologist asked Linda what she thought about her ability and problem. She shrugged her shoulders and said she didn't know, a frequent initial response by children to early ecosystemic questioning. The consultant presented his diagnosis, motivational deficit disorder, and attributed the problem to confusion and differing perceptions and expectations among the adults, as well as overprotective, "special" adult treatment of Linda. He did his best to show appreciation for everyone's efforts, but recommended that the adults shift their thinking from intrapsychic to interactional, and that they ask Linda to do her work, since all professional tests had indicated she was capable. The consultant asked Linda what she thought of his ideas. She said she agreed. A two-week system of home consequences for school behavior was instituted. Immediately after the first session, the school psychologist revealed to the consultant that the reading specialist thought that Linda might be schizophrenic or psychotic in addition to learning disabled.

Results

The results of the intervention with Linda were impressive. Following the first session, she gradually began to pay more attention and to do more of her work. She acted and spoke more her age. At one point in the second session, the consultant spontaneously interrupted the adult conversation and said to Linda, "What's six times three?" Linda replied, "eighteen," without a second's hesitation. The reading specialist, unfortunately, had left the meeting and missed this vignette. It was also after this specialist's departure that the consultant recommended the discontinuance of special tutoring for Linda. The school psychologist processed this recommendation later with the specialist, and although the suggestion was not well received by the specialist, the school psychologist and the consultant hoped that an "interactional seed" would eventually take root and grow. After some further discussion, the family and school participants decided that they were on the right track and would continue the current approach until some problem developed. Linda continued to improve and even excel academically the rest of the school year and the following year. No follow-up family therapy or marital therapy were needed in this case.

Discussion

The circumstances of Linda's case are very common, unfortunately. Intrapsychic thinking pervades our culture, schools, and families.

But a shift in that thinking and practice can have dramatically positive results. Such a shift can also be controversial and cause trouble. In this case, the school psychologist had to confront the reading specialist privately to recommend a different approach. Although the specialist had been given similar advice before, she continued to be resistant and to hold to her way of thinking. As is discussed elsewhere in this book, school personnel and other professionals and leaders sometimes have strong commitments to the intrapsychic model, often because of unresolved personal issues in their own families. Intrapsychic thinking and practice from such important people wreaks extensive devastation on our interpersonal, social, and cultural landscape. Great leadership—defined as caring, vision, and courage—especially from school superintendents, principals, and other administrators, is required if children, families, and society are to be better served.

The Neurobiological Disease

Background

Michael, eleven, had been hospitalized earlier in the year for what was diagnosed as suicidal ideation and was currently in a self-contained sixth-grade classroom designed to give children specialized attention. He had previously spent about six weeks in each of two well-known psychiatric centers. At the first center, the staff had put him on a strong dose of a popular antidepressant medication; at the second facility, the staff had gradually reduced the dosage. Both hospitals, and other psychiatric and educational professionals, had supported a diagnosis for Michael of a "neurobiological disease." When Michael had begun to show "suicidal" signs again in sixth grade, the school social worker arranged a collaborative team intervention.

Assessment and Intervention

Prior to agreeing to meet with the whole team, Michael's mother requested a private meeting with the school social worker and the ecosystems consultant to discuss the philosophy and procedures of the collaboration program. It became clear that the mother was overly protective of Michael, her only child, even against her husband's efforts to elicit more effort from him. This mother described her husband as somewhat rigid and gruff in his interactions with Michael until the consultant suggested that, perhaps, he was resistant to attending meetings at school. At that point, the mother became hostile toward the consultant and protective of her husband. The mother left this meeting in a huff, but a call from the school social worker was successful in getting both parents to return to school for a collaborative meeting with school personnel.

After hearing teacher reports at the first collaborative team intervention session attesting to Michael's psychological normalcy and ability, the consultant suggested that it was his opinion that Michael's mother's and father's interactions were probably the main cause of his problems. The consultant suggested that their belief in the "neurobiological disease" concept was interfering with their expectations of normal performance from Michael. He suggested that his impression, based on what he had heard from school personnel and observed at this meeting, was that Michael was quite normal, very bright and creative, and that he was internalizing low self-esteem from the incorrect diagnoses and treatment of the "professionals" he had been exposed to. The consultant suggested that if there were any disease Michael may have contracted, it was one resulting from exposure to "psychiatric mismanagement."

Although the parents were quite perturbed with the school consultant, and upset that his assessment contradicted the judgment of other professionals whom they respected, they agreed to "experiment with" being less protective of Michael and expecting normal behavior and achievement in school. Arrangement was made for regular, daily communication between home and school regarding Michael's performance. Michael indicated that he wasn't sure if he was normal, but that he would try to behave like normal children, that is, do his work and be sociable. He did think his parents were too protective. The parents were given a copy of my manual on interactive and motivational ideas, *Parenting by Automatic Pilot*, to read at home.

Results

After this one collaborative meeting, Michael's behavior, effort, and achievement improved dramatically. The parents were amazed. Michael was very pleased with himself. There were no signs of suicidal ideation. Three collaboration sessions were held in all following the initial meeting with the mother. All meetings took place within four weeks. Plans were instituted to fully mainstream Michael in the near future. At a one year follow-up, Michael was continuing to improve, and the parents were very happy. They continued in ongoing individual and family therapy with a therapist of their choosing.

Discussion

School-based and ecosystemic collaborative intervention with a child and his family can help to correctly identify most child home and school problems, even suicidal ideation, as primarily interactional and motivational, not psychiatric or "neurobiological." The private, confidential, and intrapsychic model of diagnosis and treatment, which is referred to here as "neuroedumedical," will predictably lead to restrictive, medicational, and residential efforts that take children out of the natural, and mainly functional, environments of home and regular classroom. The ecosystemic collaborative approach can head these destructive procedures off at the pass and find the missing piece of the puzzle without resorting to bizarre hypotheses and behavior.

Summary

Many of the children referred to collaborative team interventions in schools have been labeled incorrectly by family, school, or community players with one intrapsychic disorder or another. When children are given these labels by experts, the parents tend to expect less of their children, overprotect them, and let them do what they want. Identifying these problems as "motivational" and dealing with these problems in a collaborative and systems-oriented school climate enhances the pace and likelihood of correct diagnosis and problem resolution. Other interactional factors, such as parental disagreements and marital problems, also frequently contribute to child problems and have to be addressed. In the cases discussed in this chapter, a generally flexible and open school environment facilitated a quick absorption of ecosystemic thinking and a high level of cooperation between family members and school staff. Involvement of community providers was minimal in these cases, since the children were elementary school students for the most part and since solutions to problems were achieved quickly through joint home and school efforts. In my experience, efforts to involve pediatricians, neurologists, and other outside experts in reframing children's problems as primarily motivational have generally not been successful.

WHEN CHILD MANAGERS DISAGREE

One of the most common scenarios confronting school-based consultants involves a clash between one parent or child manager who overprotects and undercontrols and the other, who underprotects and overcontrols. In these situations, one parent or child manager expects a lot of the child and becomes very negative and abusive in the effort to make the child perform. The other child manager, instead of, or in addition to, fighting the other adult directly, resorts to protecting the child from what is perceived as the other's "abuse," and inadvertently gives the child covert permission to misbehave or underachieve. The adult conflict in these situations may be between a mother and a grandparent, or between a parent and a teacher, or among members of a school educational team. Children in these situations are quite torn and, usually, show a mixed and inconsistent pattern of good and bad behavior, which results in continued conflict between the parents. The stories that follow describe school-based efforts to restructure the family dynamics, parent management style, and family-school relationship when adults disagree as to what is best for a child.

Intergenerational Patterns

Background

Peter, nine, in fourth grade, was underachieving in school. He was shy and withdrawn, and regularly "forgot" to do his homework. Extensive efforts to help him learn apparently simple skills were only partially, and inconsistently, successful. There was much speculation among school staff about learning disabilities and low intelligence, though no test results, thus far, were conclusive. Peter had a younger sister, five, who was behaving normally in school but was a "brat" at home. Peter's parents were high achievers. His father was a rather strict, no-nonsense, type; his mother seemed a bit more accepting. Both were upset at the lack of progress of school and family efforts to improve Peter's performance.

Assessment and Intervention

Peter, his parents and sister, Peter's teacher, his sister's teacher, the school psychologist, the principal, and the ecosystems consultant were assembled for the first collaboration session. After listening to everyone's explanation and after observing a very sheepish Peter, the consultant asked about the level of agreement between the mother and father on parenting. The mother smiled and discussed her disagreement with the father's overly punitive style. The father smiled, too, and mildly defended his approach on the basis of how he was raised and how frustrated he was with Peter's behavior. Both parents had already entertained the possibility that Peter's symptoms were purposeful, that is, a retaliatory action against the father's demanding and controlling behavior. The father, though frustrated, indicated that he was open to another approach.

The ecosystems consultant proceeded to diagnose the child as overcontrolled and recommended a pulling back of parental control and more working with Peter in mutual problem-solving efforts. The consultant asked Peter whether he thought he had a problem and what he would like to do about it. Peter indicated that he thought he did have a problem and that he did not like his father's punitive tactics. Peter spoke in a low voice, slowly and reluctantly.

He seemed scared and angry. When asked about his feelings, he admitted that he was angry at his father. The father, somewhat embarrassed and angry himself, was nevertheless willing to listen. He had heard similar criticism of his behavior from his wife for years.

It was decided to try a two-week experiment during which Peter would be in charge of his own work. No punishments would be applied for school behavior. Instead, Peter and his parents would monitor Peter's successes and difficulties, and his parents would be available as consultants to Peter in his attempts to solve his own problems. A daily report card was set up so that Peter and his parents would receive daily feedback on how Peter was doing. Although school success was defined as Peter's job, the daily report card was used to guard against the possibility of Peter doing nothing for two weeks, out of habit. Another safeguard was the subtle reference by the therapist to "other measures" that might be needed if Peter was unable to manage his own work.

Results

The results of the collaborative intervention with Peter were excellent. Peter began immediately to demonstrate more responsible behavior at school. He did more and higher quality homework, took home his report cards, and was observed by his teacher to be happier and more spontaneous than before. Peter was also more cooperative and happier at home. A second and third session were held with this family during which some minor refinements in the operation of the plan were discussed, as were other disagreements between Peter's mother and father. To allow for greater honesty among the adults, the children were sent back to class when the "adult" issues became the focus of the session.

Discussion

Peter's academic problems and passive-aggressive behavior were not primarily individual or intrapsychic, but interactional, caused and maintained by parental disagreements about parenting and other issues and by the father's overcontrolling style. A switch to interactional thinking and recommendations enabled everyone to succeed in releasing Peter to do good work. As Peter began to show his ability, the family was also released to turn its attention to the "brat" behavior of the undercontrolled five-year-old daughter and the marital issues of the parents.

The family was referred by the school for therapy. They attended seven private office sessions with the school consultant over the next one and a half years to stabilize successful, but fragile, behavior patterns and to work through some of the parents' marital and family-of-origin issues. Through school and private sessions, Peter's father was able to better understand his own father's controlling and punitive parenting style and to make conscious improvements in the ways he would be a father to his son. By being a part of this collaborative intervention, teachers and other school staff were able to provide valuable information about Peter, support the parents in their efforts to look at their own behavior, and learn family intervention techniques that they could apply to other situations. The parents and school staff were also able to develop a closer relationship, which would help them work together in the future.

"The King of the Castle"

Background

Jay, fourteen, a ninth grader, was uninterested in school academics. He spoke in a sarcastic, cynical tone and seemed angry and sullen. Jay's father had a private business; his mother was a housewife and had an active interest in ceramics. Jay's brother was ten, a fifth grader, and also undermotivated at school, though less severely. The parents had both had somewhat negative school experiences and had had conflicts previously with Jay's teachers. School efforts to motivate Jay were not succeeding, and he was referred to the family-school collaboration program.

Assessment and Intervention

The first collaboration meeting was attended by Jay, his brother, his parents, his special education teachers, the director of special education, an assistant principal, the school social worker, the younger brother's guidance counselor, and the school consultant. Upon hearing the parents talk and interact with Jay, it became clear to the consultant that Jay was angry at his parents and at school officials and that the parents disagreed with each other about parenting and other matters. He also noted the similarity between Jay's cynical style and that of his parents. The consultant's diagnosis was motivational deficit disorder stemming from alternating overcontrol and undercontrol by his parents, contaminated by the mother's overprotectiveness in reaction to her husband's underprotective temper tantrums with the children. Jay's disruptive behavior in school was also being fueled by the inability of school staff to see the good in Jay and to develop a positive and supportive relationship with the parents.

The prescription for change was a more nurturing approach to Jay by the father and the negotiation between Jay and his parents of an agreement regarding school behavior and performance. In three subsequent collaboration sessions and one private office session, the parental conflicts over parenting and general control issues were discussed. The father was a bit of an autocrat, and the mother dealt with him by withdrawing and retaliating indirectly. Though there was some improvement in Jay's behavior, the issues had not been resolved when the family discontinued therapy by failing to call for another appointment, as promised.

No further contact occurred between family and consultant/therapist, nor between school and therapist for seven months. The acceptance of the collaboration model was tenuous at this particular high school, and the lack of school follow-up with the consultant was not surprising. One week before the end of the school year, however, the younger brother's name was brought up by a teacher in a casual conversation with the school social worker and consultant at the elementary school the boy attended. Through this conversation, the consultant, who had been visiting the school on behalf of another student, discovered that Jay and his brother were experiencing more trouble than ever.

A collaboration session was convened at the elementary school, but high school officials declined to attend. It was learned at this meeting that Jay's parents had originally agreed with the consultant's suggestions several months ago, but that when Jay's behavior did not improve quickly enough at school, the school officials had referred Jay for psychological testing at a nearby city hospital. The parents reported that they had been very unhappy with this process and that they had demanded afterward that Jay be returned to regular mainstream classes. A state of severe conflict had ensued between the family and the high school.

Over the next four months, several family and marital therapy sessions were held at the therapist's private office. Jay's and his brother's behavior were again a significant focus, but the principal work centered on the marital relationship.

Results

Jay's father was quite resistant to giving up his place as the "king of the castle," and was quietly furious about the increasing assertiveness of his wife—which was recommended and encouraged by the therapist. He refused to attend the last few office sessions. Jay's behavior, and his brother's, did gradually improve. His mother learned to be less protective of Jay and more controlling with her husband, who gradually got used to the "new and improved" family structure.

Discussion

Jay and his brother were modeling the disrespectful and cynical behavior of their father, the conflicts between the parents over parenting and other issues, and the competitive family-school relationship when they misbehaved at school. The parents' school experiences had been somewhat negative, and they were in part acting out their own revenge against authority through their children. The primary mechanism of change was the mother's insistence on more respectful behavior by the father. The school collaboration program was the vehicle for the introduction of the family to the therapist/consultant, but the good initial effects of this introduction were cancelled by the school's abandonment of the ecosystemic collaborative approach and referral of Jay to psychological testing, an action opposite to the approach of the consultant, who had labeled the problem as ecosystemic and interactional. Fortunately, the collaboration program was more functional at the district's elementary school. Through that school, the family was reconnected to the consultant and got the help it needed. It is unfortunate that in both of these schools, the leadership was not receptive to the idea of changing the behavior of teachers and other school staff in the direction of more honest, open, and accepting communication with families. The collaboration program in this district was eventually discontinued and the schools increased their reliance on individual assessment and intervention, that is, the diagnostic layaway plan.

It is important to note that family therapy in this case might have started seven months earlier than it did, and that when it finally did occur, it was through a chance meeting with a school staff member. Help for children cannot, of course, be expected to proceed in such haphazard circumstances. For a collaboration program to work, there must be clear commitment to the use of the model and a strong resistance to abandoning its use in favor of less demanding, traditional intrapsychic procedures, such as psychological testing, when family dynamics are the obvious cause. (The "politics" of collaboration will be dealt with in Chapter Eleven.)

The "Wicked" Stepmother

In some situations, the conflict over parenting can be between the divorced mother and father or between a biological parent and his second spouse, a stepparent. Both of these conflicts were present in the following case.

Background

Kathlin, twelve, had been underachieving in school for a few years, and now, in seventh grade, she was doing poorly or failing in all her subjects. Her sister, Barbara, fifteen, was doing well in her tenth-grade school work, but was disrespectful and unmanageable in both her mother's and father's homes. (The girls lived approximately half-time with each parent.) Teachers and other school officials had tried unsuccessfully to motivate Kathlin by working with her individually and through informal contact with her parents.

Assessment and Intervention

A collaborative team intervention was scheduled, which involved both biological parents, the stepmother, and various teachers and other school representatives. Kathlin presented a very surly and defiant attitude in the first session. Barbara acted like an innocent bystander who was annoyed at being taken out of class, since she was doing well in school. She minimized any suggestion of home problems. In addition to child problems, it was clear that the parents, though cordial and cooperative, did have a history of conflict, and that the stepmother, in particular, was annoyed at the lax attitude of the biological parents toward the girls' disrespectful, and otherwise unacceptable, behavior patterns. It was suggested at this meeting that the girls did need stricter management. The parents all agreed. The girls were asked their opinions of the situation and whether they felt it was unfair. They were mildly critical of the father and stepmother, who were stricter than their mother.

After an unsuccessful week in which Kathlin had asked and agreed to improve on her own, a daily report card was set up for her, with an agreement that poor school behavior would result in time on the bed at home—fifteen minutes for every poor grade on homework, classwork, effort, and conduct in any subject. The parents were asked to continue to work on their communication and consistency with each other.

Results

The intervention with Kathlin was very successful. After testing the resolve of her parents to follow through consistently with negative consequences, she began to do her work and, in fact, did very well in school. Problems continued at home, however, and the family requested follow-up treatment with the school consultant. In these sessions, the stepmother's anger became the main issue. She was quite bitter about her husband's failure to take a stronger stand with his ex-wife over the girls' behavior, and with his general withdrawal from her into alcohol abuse, depression, and obsession with his computer. This stepmother also had a six-year-old son from a previous marriage whom she thought the father ignored. At the time of this writing, therapy was being directed at resolving the conflicts between the father and his second wife as well as conflicts between the father and the girls' biological mother.

Discussion

Children's behavior is most often caused and maintained by conflicts between or among adult managers of children. In the case of Kathlin and Barbara, a stepmother was an important part of the interactional conflict. In response to the girls' behavior problems, the school provided an inviting context for dealing with a problem primarily rooted in family interactions. The opinions given by school personnel provided support for a firmer treatment of Kathlin, but also for the resolution of adult conflicts and the triangulated battles between various members of the family. The family developed confidence in the consultant during school sessions, which facilitated their requesting private family therapy with him two weeks after the last collaborative session at school. The ongoing relationship between the school and the consultant provided an opportunity for frequent communication between all the players in this situation. The family members not only agreed to school-therapist communication, they enthusiastically supported it.

The Depressed Teenager

Background

Henry was thirteen, an eighth grader in the middle school, and a veteran of two placements in psychiatric residential treatment facilities in the past two years. During his most recent stay, he was given antidepressant medication and treated primarily intrapsychically. Henry's mother and father were divorced and were antagonistic toward one another. The mother was currently suing the father for custody. Henry had a younger brother, a sixth grader, who was also an underachiever and a behavior problem. Since his return to school two weeks prior to the collaborative team intervention, Henry had reverted to his pattern of disrespect, skipping classes, and acting "weird." The middle school administration and the mother were on the verge of placing him in a permanent residential facility, when school officials reluctantly agreed to a meeting with the ecosystems consultant hired by the school district. No previous collaborative work had been conducted at this particular middle school because the administrators were opposed to the program for reasons that were unclear.

Assessment and Intervention

The first and only collaborative session was attended by Henry, his parents, all of his teachers (who stayed for ten-minute periods two to three at a time), the case worker from the Department of Child and Youth Services (DCYS), the middle school social worker, a guidance counselor, the principal, and the ecosystems consultant. Throughout the discussion of Henry's problem, Henry sat, looking down, apparently in a mood that combined morose, angry, and manipulative feelings. He appeared to be trying to look "psychotic" or at least strange. Teachers gave accounts of Henry's behavior that revealed his positive and sane responsiveness to firm direction. The consultant already knew, from previous experience, that the mother was seriously overprotective, undercontrolling and, in general, ineffective as a parent. Her main interest seemed to be getting revenge against her ex-husband for leaving her. Although the father was a recovering drug addict, he was the more balanced and effective parent. Unfortunately, he would probably lose the custody battle.

The consultant diagnosed Henry's problem as primarily a motivational deficit disorder, not a psychiatric disorder, and said that it stemmed mainly from the mother's ineffective parenting and the ongoing conflict between the parents. He prescribed negative home consequences for Henry's negative school behavior. He also prescribed a switch from the intrapsychic diagnostic approach and treatment plan currently in use at the middle school and at the psychiatric center (where Henry continued to go for individual therapy and increasing doses of medication). Continuing, the consultant recommended the abandonment of the residential placement

plan since Henry was not "sick," but a "pain in the neck," and
recommended a return to school where the teacher's already effective
work could be supported by family-school collaboration. Finally,
the consultant recommended that Henry look up at the meeting.
The father instructed Henry to look up, which he did instantly,
showing clear respect for the father. The meeting ended with everyone promising to think about the consultant's recommendations.
Both parents indicated that they would call the consultant for private family therapy.

Results

The following brief account of what transpired after the first and
only family-school collaboration meeting on Henry's behalf sheds
light on the strength of the intrapsychic grasp on schools, psychiatric facilities, and other institutions in American society. It also
illuminates the obstacles in the way of the adoption of an ecosystemic collaborative model of child and family intervention.

   Within twenty-four hours after the high school collaboration
session with Henry, Henry's mother reported the details of the meeting to Henry's residential facility therapist. Outraged at the pro-
ceedings, the therapist complained to the middle school principal,
and he, in turn, complained to the consultant. The principal asked
the consultant to call the irate therapist and try to address his complaints since, he said, "we have to work with these people." The
consultant predicted total failure in his ability to communicate with
the therapist, but agreed to call.

   The consultant telephoned the therapist, identified himself
and stated his wish to communicate on the matter of Henry and the
school meeting. The therapist responded by vigorously attacking
the consultant, accusing him of being "the most unethical person"
he had ever heard of. The therapist indicated that it was impossible
to make a clinical judgment of a youth based on one session at a
school and without extensive medical analysis and reports, that
Henry was severely disturbed and depressed, and that he very much
needed ongoing medication and individual therapy in order to develop a trusting relationship with the therapist. He angrily asked
for the consultant's credentials, made a vague reference to a lawsuit,

rebuffed all attempts by the consultant to discuss the situation, and eventually hung up.

The mother continued "babying" the eighth grader. The intrapsychic school, home, and therapy plan continued, and the consultant was dismissed from the case by the middle school because of the mother's unwillingness to cooperate. Efforts by the father, the middle school social worker, the pupil services director, and the consultant to get the mother to think more interactionally and to face her underlying personal problems were unsuccessful. A year later, the younger middle school child in this family was admitted to a psychiatric center as well. Most recently the mother admitted herself to the psychiatric unit of a local hospital for depression.

Discussion

The problems encountered in the attempt at a collaborative intervention on behalf of Henry are very familiar to ecosystems consultants. To break through and affect the severe dysfunction in a family such as Henry's, school leaders' commitment to the program must be firm. Their leadership has to involve taking politically charged positions against intrapsychically and economically driven professionals, agencies, and institutions.

Summary

The four case studies presented in this chapter involved disagreements between parents or between family members and school personnel regarding child diagnosis and treatment. The school-based collaborative team interventions in each case focused on identifying and changing parenting and marital behaviors that were maintaining the child problems. The school provided the forum for the discussion of conflicting viewpoints and for an ecosystemic analysis of the problems. In each case the commitment of school personnel to learning and using ecosystemic procedures was significantly linked to success or failure of the effort.

9

UNDERINVOLVED FATHERS
OR
OTHER FAMILY MEMBERS

Whether parents are married, single, or divorced, fathers are often "the missing ingredient in child success." In the case of divorce, when primary care parents (usually mothers) have children who are acting out at home or at school, it is appropriate and helpful to contact the fathers of these children and to involve them in collaborative interventions. Some of these fathers may have let relations with their children lapse, but, in general, they will agree to come to the school when they are asked, even when they live out of state, and they will usually become more actively and positively involved with their children and ex-wives. Sometimes, the fathers show initial interest only to resume their distant and dysfunctional status fairly quickly. Less frequently, the mother is underinvolved, or both parents are remote from the children. In either case, efforts need to be made to draw them in. In every case I know of, children have been better off as a result of school efforts to engage the underinvolved parent.

Child Abuse in the Name of Therapy

Background

In this case, Charles, who was twelve, and his brother, who was eight, each had his own therapist. The boys had been going to weekly individual therapy sessions for two years. The mother also occasionally visited one or the other of these therapists, usually alone, to hear reports on the children's progress. The mother also saw her own therapist once a week. The children had been placed in therapy because of their misbehavior at home and at school, but no parent-child or family therapy had taken place, nor did any of the therapists attempt to contact the school. When Charles's behavior at school failed to improve, the school psychologist referred him to the family-school collaboration program.

Assessment and Intervention

When the mother reported her intention to utilize the school's collaboration program to the children's therapists, they both expressed concern. Charles's therapist called the school and insisted on interviewing the school consultant before giving "approval" of the collaborative effort to his "patient's" mother. He requested that the interview be held without the mother present so that he would not violate his patient's confidentiality to the mother. This "private" meeting was scheduled by the school psychologist, without the mother's consent, and when the mother was told about it, she showed up at the meeting. The therapist, who had worked with this mother and her child for two years, was very upset with her "inappropriate" behavior, and asked her to leave. The school principal, disregarding the advice of the consultant, acceded to the therapist's wishes and also asked the mother to leave. The principal was apparently afraid to alienate this therapist, who was not only a child mental health practitioner but also her neighbor.

After the mother left, the therapist attempted to control the meeting, explain and defend his approach to therapy, minimize the lack of results in two years, and express negativity regarding the use of the collaborative program, which he viewed as a "conflicting" approach. While the principal attempted to avoid conflict, the school psychologist and the boy's teacher argued for the collaboration program, the consultant explaining his approach as calmly as he could. This was extremely difficult, since the consultant's approach to therapy was, in fact, virtually opposite to the therapist's. The therapist left the meeting, reluctantly agreeing to "allow" the therapy, but indicating his desire to have a report that would help him decide whether he could continue to "treat his patient" under these circumstances. It should be noted that Charles's mother had not asked the therapist to investigate the collaborative program, but had agreed to let him do so at his request. She had not anticipated that the therapist would actually schedule an investigative school meeting without her present. In addition, the therapist told the school team to be very careful of this mother because she was a "borderline personality."

Several days after the meeting with the therapist, the collaborative team held its first collaborative team intervention. After hearing from school staff about Charles's behavior, and after observing Charles in the session (he was totally silent and uncooperative), the consultant recommended that the mother administer stiffer consequences. The teacher reported that Charles was abusive to other students in class, did not do his homework, and was disrespectful to the teacher. The mother's behavior showed her to be a caring person who gave her son every opportunity to speak his mind. The son's school behavior was diagnosed by the consultant as "brat" behavior stemming from undercontrol and overprotection by the mother. The consultant also stated his surmise that the private therapist had added to the problem by giving the impression that it would require years to discover and fix it. The younger brother showed no school problems, but he was a "brat" at home.

When asked about the boys' father, the mother expressed great negativity and said she did not want him involved. Because of the consultant's and school staff's encouragement and persistence, however, she eventually agreed to include him. The father traveled from his home in another part of the country to attend the second collaboration session. The tension was thick in the room as the parents traded insults and accusations. The mother was furious at the father for "using her for five years until he found someone better." The father claimed that he had told her from the beginning that he didn't love her. When the marital bitterness began to escalate, the consultant asked the parents' permission to send the children back to class. The parents agreed. Soon after this, the mother threatened to walk out of the meeting, but was convinced to stay. She felt very victimized, she said, and disliked what she perceived as her ex-husband's "smug attitude." The father was angry at his wife's "self-pity." Through perseverance, gentleness, and straight talk, the school staff found a way to get the parents to calm down and focus on the welfare of the children. The parents agreed that the boys needed more control. The father was harder to convince, probably in part because of his guilt about leaving his children and moving in with a new family out of state. Both parents agreed to try to communicate and to use the consultant as a mediator when necessary.

The next session was a private office session attended only by the school consultant and the mother. She was initially very angry about the involvement of the father, but gradually calmed down. While the mother was in the office, the consultant telephoned the father at his home out of state and elicited from him a cooperative attitude. The third meeting was also a private office session, this time with the mother, the consultant, and the children. The mother agreed to take stronger measures in response to the children's misbehavior, and the consultant told the children they would only have to come back to therapy (something they were sick of) if they did not behave. The boys predicted they would not be back. They did come back the following week, however, because of some continued opposition, but the mother and the teacher reported great improvement on Charles's part. The younger brother, who was only slightly improved, became the major focus of therapy.

Results

Six weeks after the private meeting with Charles's therapist, both Charles and his brother were much improved. This occurred after two years of individual therapy for both children, with no improvement. The boys' father continued to stay involved; he even called the consultant/therapist from out of state to ask his advice on whether to support his ex-wife's withholding a Christmas present from Charles pending his behavior report from school. The consultant advised him to support his ex-wife and he did. At the end of the school year, the teacher reported a dramatic turnaround in Charles.

Discussion

Sending children to individual therapy is usually not a good idea. In this case, the therapists for Charles and his brother were abusing the children and the family by giving the impression that the children were getting better. They weren't. When the father had called Charles's individual therapist in the early stages of that therapy, the therapist had advised the father to stay away from his son and said that it was bad for his son to have contact with a father who was so far away and at whom the mother was angry. The therapist thought contact with the father would cause too much conflict for the son. In the collaborative ecosystemic model, the belief is quite the opposite. By bringing the father and mother to school, the school team was able to help them work through the tension and conflict and reestablish a working relationship that was in the best interests of the children.

The City Boy

Background

Mark, fifteen, a ninth grader, had recently transferred from a city high school to a rural one. Within one week of his arrival, Mark had developed some peer conflicts and had gotten into a physical fight. After discussions with Mark and his parents, it appeared that there was a substantial parent-child conflict between Mark and his mother, and between Mark and his biological father. Both Mark and his mother had been physically abused by the father, from whom Mark's mother was now seeking a divorce. The family was referred for collaborative team intervention.

Assessment and Intervention

The first collaborative session was attended by Mark and his two sisters, ages nine and six, his mother, his father, all his major-subject teachers, the school social worker, the school psychologist, the assistant principal, and the ecosystems consultant. Through the various comments and interactions of the participants, it became clear that the mother had a short and explosive temper, and that the mother and Mark were very angry at the father. The father seemed to have his temper under control. The consultant diagnosed Mark's behavior problem as primarily motivational, stemming from both his parents' problems with temper, their continued anger with each other, and other parenting dysfunctions. The parents were advised to stay calm, work out consistent home and school guidelines with input from Mark, and to work together on parenting Mark. The parents seemed receptive and agreed to follow the advice given. The school social worker suggested that the family might call the consultant and see him privately if the problems continued.

Three weeks later, Mark's parents, Mark, and his sisters began private family therapy with the consultant, which focused on management of Mark's continuing unruly behavior. Eight sessions were held with the family over the next four months, with moderate progress. In the next year, Mark's mother was called by the school because of teacher complaints about Mark's disrespectful behavior. A collaborative team intervention was held at the high school to coordinate home, school, and therapist efforts.

Thirty more sessions were held over the next eight months. In response to Mark's continued resistance to joint parenting and school efforts, he was eventually placed in a self-contained classroom in school. He was also sent to the home of his father, who had recently moved out, when his mother couldn't control him. Communication between home, school, and consultant remained frequent during the time of therapy. Mark was sent to his father's house for one to five days at a time, contingent upon his level of unmanageability at his mother's house. Mark's sisters also began to act up in similar ways, and collaborative interventions were initiated at the younger child's elementary school.

Results

Despite many ups and downs during the therapy process, Mark did gradually make progress, as did his sisters. He became more respect-ful, and complied with the "consequences" imposed by his parents for unacceptable behavior—lying on his bed or going to his father's home. He became more respectful of teachers and was gradually phased back into the regular education classes. Mark became closer to his father, his mother became more calm and patient, and the relationship between Mark's parents improved, though they pro-ceeded in the direction of divorce.

Discussion

Mark had been an abused child and was continuing to be abused. He was underprotected and overcontrolled by both parents, but in-consistently overprotected by his mother against her husband and against her own efforts to keep him under control. The mother felt great guilt about Mark's past and wanted to make it up to him. He had developed a self-protective aggression, similar to his father's, which also served to express his frustration and anger. The princi-pal mechanisms of change were his mother's adoption of a calmer, but forceful, parenting style, and Mark's reconciliation with his father. These outcomes were accomplished through family therapy and through a close collaboration between family, school, and ther-apist that was initiated by the school.

The Boy Who Wanted to Live with His Father

Background

Jacques, twelve, underachieving and misbehaving at school, had been begging to live with his biological father for five years. Each time, his mother said no. She had divorced her alcoholic husband and was remarried to a very stable professional man. The ex-husband was recovering, but the mother didn't trust him. There was a younger brother, seven, who felt fine living with his mother. Jacques was referred to a collaborative team intervention.

Assessment and Intervention

In the first collaborative session with the mother and her second husband present, it was clear that this second husband was angry at Jacques, and that the mother was in the middle. The stepfather took it very personally that he was being rejected by his stepson and retaliated by being mean. When the mother tried to protect her son, the stepfather would get angrier at the son. The consultant recommended that Jacques' father be called at his out-of-state residence and asked to attend a collaborative session at school. He was very cooperative, said he loved his son, and agreed to come to a session.

The second collaborative session was held one week later. The similarity between Jacques and his father was striking. The father was a rough and ready type, with dirt under his fingernails and a blue-collar job. He had done very little in school as a child. He took Jacques hunting when they were together. It was clear that Jacques' mother and stepfather did not like Jacques' father, and they had not communicated with him regarding Jacques' school performance. We asked the biological parents to begin to cooperate more, and especially for the mother to speak to Jacques' father directly, not to go through her son.

Jacques had run away from the first collaboration session with his stepdad, but he willingly came to the second one, with his father present. He said that he wanted to live with his father and his father agreed. Prior to this time, Jacques' father had been putting him off. Because things were not improving with Jacques, his mother tearfully agreed to let him go. A third collaborative session was scheduled for a week hence to give everyone a chance to reconsider the decision. At this next meeting, everyone agreed to go ahead with the plan.

Results

Jacques did move in with his father immediately. Follow-up over the next few months indicated that things were going well for Jacques and his father, and that his mother and her family were doing well also.

Discussion

Stepfamilies are a more and more common phenomenon. When one parent remarries, children may wish to live with the other parent. Gender identification may also play a role, with boys sometimes wanting to live with their fathers and girls with their mothers. In the case of Jacques, it is hard to determine whether he just missed his father or felt driven away by a rigid, demanding stepfather. In any case, family-school collaboration played a constructive role in facilitating a solution to the problem.

Abandoned by Both Parents

Background

Donald, thirteen, was a major behavior problem at home and school—he basically did whatever he wanted. Donald had been abandoned by his alcoholic father when he was a year old. His mother had remarried, but her second husband was given to anger and occasional alcoholic rages. Donald's mother had trouble protecting him from his stepfather. Donald was seven when his grandparents offered to have him live with them in another state, and his mother had agreed. Donald's individual therapist, whom he had seen from age three, concurred with the move. Although Donald was happy to be away from his stepfather, he missed his mother. His grandparents considered him depressed and sent him to therapists; he had seen his most recent one for the three years prior to referral to the family-school collaboration program. The therapist had diagnosed childhood depression and post-traumatic stress disorder related to his abuse by his father and stepfather in the first seven years of his life. Despite all the therapy, Donald was worse than ever.

Assessment and Intervention

The first collaboration session was attended by Donald, his grandparents, various school officials, the school consultant, his private therapist, and his mother, who traveled several hundred miles from another state to attend the meeting. Although the mother had been invited to the meeting, she had not been expected to come, and her arrival was a surprise to everyone present.

After listening to everyone's comments, the consultant suggested that "brat syndrome" and motivational deficit disorder were more appropriate diagnoses than one focusing on early childhood trauma. The consultant reasoned that Donald had had years to get over early traumas. He did agree, however, that Donald was probably suffering from depression and anger related to continued abandonment by his mother and conflict between his mother and grandmother over parenting styles. The mother favored a stricter approach than the grandparents, who were tolerant of Donald because of his "psychological" problem. The consultant said that higher expectations would be appropriate for Donald and recommended possibly reuniting him with his mother, in conjunction with his mother's agreement to keep her second husband under control. The grandmother was somewhat annoyed at the consultant's assessment, perhaps because it contradicted her current thinking or because it favored the idea of Donald's leaving her. The private therapist was supportive of the consultant's analysis, and agreed that some further ingredient was necessary in the recipe for child success. Donald agreed that he should be better behaved, but wasn't sure what to do about where to live. He frequently showed tears during the session.

Results

The one-session collaboration intervention was quite effective. After much discussion in the family, following this meeting, it was agreed that Donald would try to live with his mother. Follow-up data are not yet available on this case because Donald had only recently moved in with his mother at the time of this writing.

Discussion

The school provides an excellent meeting place for child caretakers and children who might not otherwise get together. In this case, a problem child, a therapist doing mainly individual therapy with the child, the grandparents who were raising the child, and the mother, living out of state and in conflict with her parents, all gathered together. An ecosystemic analysis helped all the players present to reframe the problem from intrapsychic to interactional, and to fashion a solution that involved restructuring current relationships rather than focusing on past traumas. The support of the school staff was probably essential to the scheduling and the success of this intervention.

Summary

Fathers are often the missing ingredient in child success. Sometimes, though less often, mothers are the missing ingredient. For various reasons, divorce among them, fathers may be merely peripheral figures, underinvolved in their children's lives. Mothers may conspire to keep it that way, perhaps with good reason. By helping fathers and mothers to get more involved with their children and to work more cooperatively with each other, family-school collaboration programs can contribute greatly to children's success in school and to their general level of happiness and self-esteem.

HELPERS OUTSIDE
THE NUCLEAR FAMILY

Probably in large part as a response to the increases in divorce and in two-career families, grandparents and other family members are playing increasingly influential roles in child rearing. Some examples of grandparents' involvement have been presented in earlier chapters. Helpful roles are also played by teachers and community personnel outside the family. This increased support is often very helpful, but sometimes there are strings of control and intrusion attached to the help. The case studies in this chapter address the actions schools can take to work with extended families and others who are willing to help with a child's problems.

Many Facets

Background

Two adult siblings, a brother and sister, whose marriages had failed, had moved back in with their parents. They each had two children who lived with them. They also had serious personal and marital problems. The children's parents and grandparents all shared in child care. The four children—two from each adult sibling—were the presenting children in this case. The interventions took place in two stages over four years.

The first intervention concerned two of the four children—Kevin, five, and his brother, Bobby, nine—who were both acting up in their school classrooms and at home. Their mother was a recovering alcoholic and drug addict. Their father, from whom the mother was divorced, lived in another state, but still had some contact with the boys.

The second intervention occurred about two years later with Kyle, eight, the oldest of the male sibling's two children. This father had also been using drugs, but was, at this time, recovering. The two children stayed alternately with their father and their mother, who lived in another town. Kyle was a behavior problem at home and in an after-school day-care program, but not in his second-grade public school classroom. He had been diagnosed with attention deficit hyperactive disorder (ADHD) and was being given Dexedrine; the dosage had recently been increased. Kyle had regular sessions with his neurologist and a child advocate, both of whom the mother trusted greatly.

Assessment and Intervention

The first collaboration session was attended by Kevin, his brother, his grandmother and grandfather, his mother, his teacher, his brother's teacher, the school psychologist, the school social worker, and the ecosystems consultant. After listening to the various accounts, the consultant diagnosed Kevin's and Bobby's problem as motivational deficit disorder stemming from their mother's undercontrol. After securing everyone's agreement with the diagnosis, the consultant recommended practicing the use of control tactics immediately, within the session. When Kevin refused to behave in response to his mother's direction to stop interrupting and to sit still, for example, his mother asked him to sit in a time-out chair away from the group. Moreover, when Kevin refused to sit in the time-out chair, the consultant guided the mother in the use of a "restraining" procedure in which Kevin was held on the floor on his back. His mother referred to the procedure as an "exorcism." Bobby was also held on the floor to show him what it would be like if he refused to behave. The mother and the grandparents were instructed to help each other in enforcing rules at home. Two more sessions were held during this first stage of intervention.

Two years later, two collaborative sessions were held with Kyle, age eight, at an elementary school different from the one attended by Kyle's cousin, Kevin. Kyle and his mother were accompanied by Kyle's grandmother and Kyle's child advocate. The meeting was also attended by Kyle's second grade teacher, the school principal, and the school consultant. After hearing everyone's opinion, the consultant diagnosed the problem as motivational deficit disorder stemming from the mother's undercontrolling and overprotecting the child. The consultant recommended discontinuing Dexedrine, abandoning the neurologist's hypotheses as a primary explanation for Kyle's misbehavior, and switching to greater reliance on child management approaches. Kyle's father attended the second collaboration session, but the mother did not.

Results

The results of multigenerational collaboration were excellent. Kevin and Bobby responded immediately to the "exorcism" approach used by their mother, who was very pleased to learn an effective method of child management. Their grandmother stopped overprotecting and undercontrolling the grandchildren and overprotecting and undercontrolling her adult children. In the intervention with Kyle, his father was able to find a more sensible control tactic than Dexedrine. Unfortunately, Kyle's mother was too influenced by neurological and advocacy experts to be able, or willing, to examine how her own issues might be affecting Kyle. Kyle did improve, however, despite the contradictory messages from his parents.

Discussion

School-based collaboration with families can provide entry into home situations that are very debilitating and that may not find their way to private office settings. In the situation presented here, two adult children of the same parents were malfunctioning as individuals and were bequeathing their problems to the next generation. The fact that help was available in their children's schools enabled the drug-abusing, divorced, and otherwise troubled adult children and their parents to make use of that help many times and in many ways. It is likely that the site of the service, namely, the school, and the team format, offer distinct advantages in the task of working with multiproblem, multigenerational families.

Letting Go

Background

Kurt, twelve, was a seventh grader who had been placed in a self-contained special education classroom because of major behavior problems and underachievement. Kurt lived with his parents, who were both drug addicts and with whom Kurt fought incessantly, verbally and sometimes physically. The parents were unemployed, had no phone, did not sign for certified mail sent to their house, and did not come to school for parent-teacher meetings. The school staff decided to refer Kurt and his parents to collaborative team intervention.

Assessment and Intervention

Through persevering efforts by the school social worker, who sent letters home with Kurt, Kurt's mother eventually attended a collaborative school meeting, but the father refused to come. It was clear at once that this mother was quite anxious and depressed, and probably had been drinking and/or using drugs very recently before the meeting. Efforts were made to educate the mother in nurturing and calm parenting methods, but there was little hope that she would be able to follow through. After a second collaborative meeting one week later, in which the mother again showed interest but little effort to change, it was decided to attempt to reach her brother, Kurt's uncle, by phone. The brother had been identified by Kurt as a very stable, reliable individual whom Kurt admired and liked.

Kurt's mother was asked to give the school permission to invite her brother to the next collaborative meeting two weeks later. At this meeting, it was arranged that Kurt would spend more time with his uncle on weekends and summer vacation.

Results

The introduction of the uncle into the family structure proved to be very beneficial to Kurt. He began to behave more appropriately and work harder at his studies. His fights with his parents continued, however, and his behavior in school fluctuated with his situation at home. Within a few months after the third collaborative session, the school social worker began to talk periodically with the uncle about the possibility of Kurt's living with him and his wife. The uncle responded very favorably to this suggestion and about one year later, Kurt's mother agreed to let Kurt live with his uncle and transfer to another school. The mother had moved away from her husband and had a new boyfriend, and the presence of this companion may have helped her to let go of her son. The increasing conflict between the boyfriend and Kurt may also have contributed to her decision; Kurt had recently destroyed some neighborhood property in a fit of rage. Kurt had only recently moved to his uncle's at the time of this writing.

Discussion

A crucial role was played in this case by the town youth officer, who came to a follow-up collaboration session and helped to convince the mother to let go of the child. He also offered to be available to her the next day at the police department to sign the papers authorizing temporary transfer of guardianship to the uncle. Another positive role was played by the special education teacher, who stressed the negative effect of Kurt's home life on his academic and behavioral success in school. Without the move to his uncle's home, Kurt was to be restricted to a half-day schedule in school because of his unmanageability. Plans were already in place to remove him to a special day school for emotionally disturbed children. In my view, Kurt's move to his uncle's home would have been much more difficult to arrange in a setting other than the school.

The Boy with Three Parents

Background

Ethan, seven, a second grader, was a behavior problem in school. His nine-year-old sister was not. The two children lived with their mother, their maternal grandmother, and the grandmother's second husband. Ethan's father lived in an adjacent town but rarely spent time with Ethan. All three of Ethan's "parents" thought the school was overreacting to Ethan's behavior in class because he was so easy to manage at home. It was also the case, however, that his mother and grandmother were arguing over how to manage Ethan. The grandmother, who had taken on most of the parenting responsibilities, was angry at her daughter for being selfish and neglecting Ethan. The stepgrandfather, who was an excellent male role model and in many ways a surrogate father to Ethan, thought his wife was too tolerant of her daughter's neglect.

Assessment and Intervention

The first contact between the family and the ecosystems consultant was in the consultant's private family therapy office. After two private sessions, he requested a collaborative team intervention at school. It was here that the conflict between family and school was discussed, and the family left this meeting with greater, but not complete, confidence in the school's opinion. Through nine additional private sessions over three months, various family issues were worked on, including the mother-daughter conflict, the family-school conflict, and the grandmother-stepgrandfather conflict. During this time, active communication between home, school, and therapist continued through the use of a daily report card and informal communication.

Results

The intervention with Ethan and his family was very successful. Following the first collaborative session, Ethan's behavior immediately improved and, after some occasional turbulence, stabilized at a high level of cooperation and achievement. After several stormy sessions, the mother and grandmother came to a greater understanding and acceptance of each other. Ethan's mother took increased interest in him and assumed more responsibility for him. The grandmother relinquished some of her authority and involvement as her daughter became more active. The grandparents spent more time together and assumed a more "fun" role with Ethan. Ethan's mother began to talk of moving out, but decided against it for financial reasons. A year later, conditions at home and school were reported as very good.

Discussion

The developing of a collaborative relationship between a family therapist and a school and the therapist's participation in school consultations can be extremely helpful to children and families. In this case, the close relationship between the consultant and the school facilitated the family's agreement to go to therapy and their further agreement to attend a collaboration session in school. Ongoing family-therapist-school contact allowed an open flow of information, feedback, and support for all the players in the situation. Finally, the importance of grandparents and, in this case, a step-grandparent, was again demonstrated.

The Boy Without a Parent

Background

Jonathan, eleven, was in fifth grade and underachieving. He already had been assigned to an in-school tutor for part of his school day, but he was not doing the homework necessary to keep up with his class. He had trouble concentrating on his work and also exhibited a lack of social responsiveness to both teachers and students. Jonathan, an only child, lived with his mother and had no contact with his father, who had disappeared nine years previously. Jonathan's mother held two jobs, but she had a break after school, and visited with Jonathan then for half an hour. After that, Jonathan was alone. He put himself to bed. This had been their pattern for two years or so, when the mother was invited into school for a collaborative meeting.

Assessment and Intervention

The first collaborative meeting was attended by Jonathan and his mother, all his teachers, including his in-school tutor, the school social worker, the guidance counselor, and the ecosystems consultant. All the school personnel reported a similar perception—that Jonathan was very polite, but seemed to have difficulty paying attention and doing his homework. His mother, who looked somewhat older than her age, had long hair tied back in a ponytail and wore a dungaree jacket with peace signs on it. She indicated a desire to be cooperative but said that she was unable to do much more than she was already doing because of her need to work two jobs. She said that she had lectured Jonathan and even lost her temper with him, but nothing seemed to work. Her attitude in the meeting gave the consultant the impression that following school rules and doing homework were not her highest priorities for her son. She indicated that she was considering asking a friend to move in with her to help with supervision of Jonathan. The consultant diagnosed Jonathan's problem as a motivational deficit disorder stemming from undercontrol and underprotection and asked the mother to attempt to provide more supervision. A daily report card was initiated, and the mother was asked to spend more time with Jonathan as well as put more effort into supervising his school work. Jonathan was to be rewarded for satisfactory performance with praise, free time, and special time with his mother.

Four collaborative meetings were held with Jonathan and his mother, but Jonathan's pattern remained unchanged. It was strongly suspected by school personnel that the mother, though agreeing to the collaboration plan, was not really implementing it. When pushed to clarify her home procedures, the mother became angry, and she refused to do anything differently. In a move unseen in several hundred other collaborative sessions, the mother abruptly left the meeting and took her son with her, vowing to transfer him to another school. Jonathan did return to school the next day, however.

Results

Jonathan's mother did not return for further meetings, although the school social worker tried to reengage her interest and maintain communication. The teachers, having witnessed the mother's behavior and having become sympathetic to Jonathan's plight, began to work more positively with him. They interpreted Jonathan's failure to comply less as an intrapsychic "attitude" problem and more as an interactional result of his circumstances. The in-school tutor, in particular, after consultation with the guidance counselor, social worker, and school consultant, began to develop a closer, more personal relationship with Jonathan and became a kind of surrogate mother. And Jonathan's mother continued to help him in her own way, since she did love him.

Through some combination of collaborative efforts, which are difficult to quantify, Jonathan improved his academic performance dramatically. Poor to failing grades in November were raised to Bs and As in June.

Discussion

Though Jonathan's mother was unwilling or unable to fully, or officially, cooperate with school efforts, some combination of home and school interventions turned Jonathan around. Perhaps Jonathan simply turned himself around after seeing how much everybody cared, or how helpless they were to help him without his cooperation. Most likely, the loving attention of the in-school tutor and other school personnel was a major factor. It seems likely, in this case, that without collaborative efforts in school on behalf of Jonathan, his pattern of underachievement and depression would have continued or deteriorated. Follow-up information will become available in the next school year.

Summary

Grandparents, uncles, other family members, neighbors, and friends can have significant effects on the lives of children and their parents, for better or worse. Stories have been told in this chapter of school-based efforts to involve people outside the nuclear family in a positive way. Different situations required different behavior on the part of the players involved. In my experience, it is sometimes necessary to seek help for children outside the immediate nuclear family, and by coordinating their efforts in school, professional helpers can improve their chances of success.

Part Four

ESTABLISHING
A
PROGRAM

11

THE POLITICS
OF COLLABORATION

The chapters in this book have thus far focused on the philosophy and mechanics of the school-based ecosystemic collaborative model. Many case examples involving collaborative team interventions have been recounted. But all of this knowledge will be gathering dust on a shelf unless school systems open their doors to this model. This chapter is concerned with ways of establishing and maintaining a collaboration program in a school or school district. Although school systems are not totally opposed to systems thinking, most educators have not been trained in it, and there are, in addition, many political, economic, and personal obstacles to be overcome.

Obstacles

The task of setting up and operating a school-based ecosystemic collaboration program may very well be extremely frustrating. My own experience with schools has taught me that most educators have been trained in the intrapsychic model of thinking and do not understand that child academic and behavior problems are principally motivational and contextual, that is, having to do with dysfunctional relationships. Educators are too often trained to use the "diagnostic layaway plan," that is, to test, label, and place students, not to work on restructuring relationships. Educators generally react to talks on ecosystems collaboration with some combination of shock, anger, denial, disbelief, and apathy. A speaker is sometimes lucky to find one person in an audience of fifty who will actually be inspired enough to begin work on establishing a program. The average "germination" time before even getting a call after a talk may be one to two years. This is true of all audiences, regardless of position—whether social workers or school principals—and regardless of the grade level these educators are working in.

Even after school social workers or other educators express great enthusiasm for the program, they may be discouraged by the many minds that are uneducated in systems thinking and hearts that are uninterested in it or afraid of controversy. Systems therapists and school coordinators who become interested in establishing an ecosystems collaboration program in schools may feel that they have strayed into a mine field. Some of the obstacles they will encounter are described below.

The first obstacle to the installation and operation of a school-based collaboration program is probably the educators' perception of their job as predominantly "academic." In schools, no one "owns" concern for the welfare of the children. Although the original one-room school house setting may have promoted a closer, more intimate relationship between teachers and parents, today's teachers seem to withdraw from nonacademic contact with students and their families. This distancing seems to increase as the child gets older. One of the factors contributing to this great divide between home and school is the presence in schools of various support services, such as guidance, school psychology, social work, and special education. Whereas, in the past, teachers may have had no choice but to discuss nonacademic issues with parents, now it has become the job of "specialists." Although the arrival of the specialists has expanded the variety of educational services schools can provide, it has also, in some instances, resulted in a decrease in regular teachers' responsibility for the overall needs of the child—including the psychological or emotional needs.

There are certainly many teachers who continue to take primary responsibility for the whole or holistic welfare of their students and who use "support services" in ways that were intended, that is, as a "support." Others, however, withdraw from the holistic role. The philosophy and procedures of the ecosystemic collaboration model run full in the face of what might be called this "partistic" approach to education, which prevails in many schools. Until frontline teachers take primary responsibility for the welfare of their students, and until those in support services are willing to work as a team, we will not be solving our crisis in American child-rearing and education.

A second, and very dominant, obstacle to the ecosystems collaborative model is, of course, the prevalence of intrapsychic thinking in schools, in other institutions serving schools, and in families. When a child is not succeeding in school or is looking glum or agitated, many teachers will ask the child, "What's wrong?" and talk with the child about problem-solving strategies. When the "problem" reveals itself to be interactional—for example, anger at, or fear of, parents—many teachers will decide that they are now "over their head" and will refer the matter to the specialist or the administrator. Many teachers are uncomfortable discussing these matters with parents. Unfortunately, these "special" educators or support personnel have also been trained primarily in an intrapsychic belief system and will primarily use the intrapsychic procedures of individual counseling, group counseling, peer counseling, and punishment (detention and suspension). Problems can be diagnosed intrapsychically as low self-esteem, poor impulse control, or developmental delay. Contacts with parents usually stop short of communication about essential subjects, for example, the level of agreement about parenting between parents and the level of peace and happiness in the home. Educators, generally trained in a destructive notion of privacy and confidentiality that outlaws helpful communication, often think these matters are "none of their business." And yet these "private" matters are the primary factors in student performance and behavior in school. The success of the ecosystems collaborative model depends on the use of communication and interactional thinking and behavior with students and families.

The lack of accountability in schools is yet a third obstacle to the adoption of an ecosystemic collaborative model. Schools do not succeed or fail on the basis of their students' achievement. All children are required to go to school, and most parents can't afford to pick and choose where they will send their children. In addition, it is difficult for most parents to determine whether a school is doing its job. There are many self-serving explanations schools can employ when a student doesn't achieve and becomes a behavior problem. Parents can be told that a child has a learning disability, is developmentally delayed, is immature, or needs a more structured setting. Parents generally do not know what these terms mean and have no way to test their truth or falsehood. If schools could more easily be tested for excellence and if they stayed "in business" only on the basis of excellence, ecosystemic collaboration would become much more popular because it works well and is cost effective.

A fourth obstacle to the collaborative model is the level of insight produced in ecosystemic collaborative discussions and meetings; educators become anxious when they realize how similar the problems in the students' families are to those in their own families. Educators are human beings, too. Most are married or divorced and have children. Many educators—even principals, superintendents, and school board presidents—have the same problems with their children and their marriages as are being discussed in the collaborative meetings. Often the individual adult problems, parent-child conflicts, and marital difficulties that come to light in the meetings resemble the teacher's conflicts with the same child. A teacher may be acting out his or her own parent-child or other conflicts on a student in the classroom. A problem in the student's family may parallel a problem in the educator's family—a matter that should not be overlooked by the prospective "collaborationist." The ability to establish and maintain a successful collaboration program requires a clear understanding of this connection and a readiness to deal with the periodic defensive, angry, and avoidant behavior of educators at all levels of the educational system, as well as that of community players, who sometimes instinctively withdraw from the intense personal emotionality generated by "looking in the mirror" in collaborative discussions and interventions.

The neuroedumedical industry presents a fifth obstacle in the form of an informal, but very tightly enmeshed, monopolistic, economically motivated system of child management that is based on intrapsychic thinking and the privacy model of child rearing. The various components of the neuroedumedical industry—institutions of education, medicine, justice, and social service—diagnose and treat children as individual clients or patients—unattached, and without family. The "neuro" in the industry title refers to the great weight this system gives to neurological diagnoses and treatments. Children are tested, labeled, and placed by officials in the "educational" and "medical" institutions, with little attention to the systems the children come from and to which they belong.

Those who would seek to arrange systems collaboration will often face a war, nothing less. There should be no illusion here. When ecosystems collaboration occurs, all those involved—children, parents, teachers, service providers, and others—become'progressively more aware that problems are not primarily intrapsychic, but motivational. And they realize that there is an alternative, less expensive, more natural way to prevent and solve child problems, that is, through mutual communication and, when necessary, consultation with an expert in child rearing and ecosystems collaboration. When this happens, the neuroedumedical industry begins to lose money and power, and professional jealousy and competitiveness become factors to be reckoned with. At this point, there will be a strong reaction from those whose jobs, status, and income rest heavily on the use of largely unnecessary educational, psychiatric, and psychological tests; psychiatric hospitalization and drug rehabilitation programs; medications and specialized medical tests; court-mandated residential treatment programs; and all varieties of intrapsychic, nonsystemic treatment programs for individual children. Efforts should be made in these situations to involve all relevant professionals in collaborative efforts, even though they may be philosophically opposed to these efforts.

There is little hope of reasoning with the officials who are in positions of power in the neuroedumedical institutions because, in addition to their financial interests being vested against ecosystemic collaboration, they themselves are intrapsychically trained and often have their own children on medication, taking tests, enlisted in hospital programs, and undergoing individual therapy. The best chance of winning the collaboration war lies in influencing the vast majority of people who know common sense when it is explained to them. This means a lot of shoe leather and talking. Eventually, a person in power can be reached who will listen to an advocate for the collaborative model.

A sixth obstacle to adoption of the collaborative model has to do with the issue of leadership in schools. Unfortunately, teachers and other educators are sometimes more interested in promotions, raises, power, comfort, public acclaim, and other matters than they are in the welfare of students. The effective use of the ecosystemic collaborative model usually requires increased effort or change on the part of educators and a willingness to do whatever is necessary for child success. The school officials who support the ecosystemic collaborative model will be taking a stand that may bring criticism and even rage reactions to their door or desk from parents, teachers, support staff, school board members, public agencies, private therapists, psychiatric facilities, and any number of other sources who take exception to the program.

Collaborative interventions in schools may also draw defensive and angry reactions from mental health professionals whose turf has been invaded by the collaboration program. Accusations may be made that the ecosystems consultant is feathering his nest by accepting into private practice clients who seek out his services following school intervention. The last case study in Chapter Eight ("The Depressed Teenager") presents a situation in which another professional opposed the viewpoint of the ecosystems consultant. It is likely that jealousy and economic threat were factors in this opposition.

Successful work with students requires adults to "look in the mirror" to see in the students' problems the reflections of adult problems and the dynamics of adult mismanagement of children. This "look" is often upsetting to adults, and some are willing to avoid it all costs, even at the cost of losing children to anger or alienation, or worse, to drugs and even suicide. The successful use of the collaboration model requires the presence of leadership qual-

ities in the personalities of its proponents. Leadership can be defined as vision, caring, and courage. Courage is not the least of
these. Those interested in ecosystemic collaborative intervention
will have to be prepared to encounter the powerful political, economic, and personal reactions of educators and other professionals.

The lack of staff training and skill in interactional thinking
and behavior constitute a seventh obstacle. To play successful collaborative roles, staff must be asked to undergo significant in-service
training—ideally as much as fifteen or twenty hours. The skills and
belief system that underlie the collaborative model are not learned
overnight by most educators. Achieving staff compliance with the
collaborative training initiatives requires leadership from school
administrators. Most teachers eventually report very positive results
from participation in the collaborative venture, but initially the
change is difficult. For some, it is something they will oppose
forever.

Money is an eighth obstacle to program installation and operation, although it is often a pseudo-issue manufactured by those
opposed to the collaborative model. While state and federal monies
are available for some training in schools, funding for training in
ecosystemic collaboration is not easily justified. Though a school
system can easily access up to $100,000 to send one so-called learning
disabled or emotionally disturbed child to a special private residential school, with dubious results, it finds it almost impossible to find
approximately $25,000 to enable a family systems consultant to work
with forty families in a year, with substantial results, and to be
available for a full year of general consultation. A school system may
claim that it is "flat broke," yet come up with hundreds of thousands
of dollars to deal with a radon or asbestos emergency.

Sometimes, however, money is a real issue, and those interested in establishing this model will need to have some suggestions
for sources of money or be able to motivate school administrators
to redirect the use of current funds to support it. An argument can
be made that utilization of the collaboration model can actually
save money through brief and effective intervention and through
the subsequent reduction in the need for further, usually more expensive, services (for example, residential placement of students
outside of the school district). Unfortunately, the obvious enormous

financial advantage of prevention over rehabilitation does not usually seem to be enough to influence the policy makers in education and government.

A ninth obstacle to the acceptance of the collaborative model is a collection of myths about ecosystemic collaboration that may be held by educators and others involved in decision making. Among these myths may be some of the following:

- Parents won't open up in large school meetings.
- Working parents—especially fathers—won't interrupt their busy schedules to come to school during their work hours.
- Parents will sue the school for defamation of character or payment for endless therapy for problems raised by school officials.
- "Real therapy" can't be done by educators.

These and other myths are often believed by educators and become obstacles to the acceptance of the collaboration approach. To "demythologize" the model, collaborationists will need to know the facts and have a variety of arguments and references in mind. For example, I have been told by several knowledgeable educational administrators that they know of no case in which a teacher has been sued by a parent for sharing observations or expressing opinions regarding a student's problem behavior. The reality is that none of these myths are true.

A final set of obstacles to the acceptance of ecosystemic collaboration has to do with the personal characteristics of the therapist/consultant. Because of the number and intensity of obstacles to school-based collaboration, its acceptance and success require in the therapist an extremely high level of energy, commitment, perseverance, patience, sensitivity, openness to criticism, genuineness, maturity, and therapeutic skill. As mentioned earlier, the school system is sometimes an educational "mine field." The active and goal-oriented collaborationist, if he or she is doing a good job, will frequently feel, and perhaps be, on the verge of rejection and expulsion from the system. The collaborative model is likely to be accepted only gradually, if at all. The collaborationist must be ready for dismissal by some schools and expect only a small percentage of schools to even consider, let alone use, the collaboration model.

A considerable amount of defensiveness, hurt, and anger can be generated in the consultant by such interactions. To be successful and avert discouragement, he or she must find ways to successfully process these reactions.

Strategies

Because of the number and strength of the obstacles to adoption of the ecosystemic collaborative model, those interested in establishing a program that is school-based must be equipped with "minesweepers" as well as an extensive and versatile arsenal of "defensive weapons." The following suggestions are presented as initial steps that those interested in establishing collaboration programs in schools may want to build on.

The first item on the consultant's agenda should be to identify and contact a school staff person who is interested in the collaborative model. This is the most important step because once this person is identified, he or she can work from within the system to arrange the introduction of the ecosystems consultant to school officials. This contact person will generally be a school social worker, school psychologist, or other support service worker. The contact may even be initiated by this school worker, who may have seen the consultant present the model at a conference, or the person may have responded to educational materials on the collaboration model sent by the consultant to the school district's pupil services or special education director. This contact person may very well eventually be the school coordinator of the program. Conversations with the contact person should focus on the specific obstacles that will be encountered in that particular school system and the best way to present the model to that particular administration.

The second step in the process should be to meet with the decision makers in a school or school district. These meetings could begin with even one decision maker, for example, a school principal, but they should ultimately include various support staff and districtwide administrators, such as the pupil personnel or special education director. More than one meeting may be necessary. The meetings are usually arranged and mediated by the school contact person and should be focused on a description of the model and discussion of its potential value to educators. Obstacles to the implementation of the program should also be covered and references offered from school coordinators of collaboration programs at other sites.

The next step should be to start a pilot program in one school. A "Ten Most Wanted" list can be constructed for referral to the program. Strategy meetings and collaborative team interventions (Steps 5 and 6 on the School Decision Chart, Figure 2.2 in Chapter Two) can be scheduled for problem students on the list. The school contact person, who probably has now become the school coordinator, should take charge of inviting all the relevant school, family, and community representatives to these meetings. The cost of the consultant's time needs to be negotiated at this time. Some free "demonstration" work may need to be offered.

A fourth step should be to inform the school faculty about the initiation of the pilot project. The ecosystems consultant should be introduced to the school staff by the principal, and a brief overall presentation on the program should be made to the assembled school staff by a team composed of the principal, the districtwide pupil services director, the school coordinator, and the ecosystems consultant. Opportunities should be given for questions and some expression of annoyance by school staff, some of whom will likely resent the introduction of a new program, particularly one that requires more contact with families. Staff should be told by their leaders that they will have ample opportunities for training in the collaboration model, and that their active participation is highly encouraged. It should be stressed that the use of the model will probably result in better student morale and performance in their classrooms.

The next phase of the process, the fifth step, should be to conduct strategy meetings and one- to three-session collaborative team interventions (CTIs) for the identified students and families. One new series of interventions might begin each week. The consultant should be available to school staff before and after CTI meetings or at other times to process any questions, objections, or comments they may have. The school coordinator should be in charge of maintaining contact with school staff and should act as a liaison among the parties.

A very important sixth step in the implementation process is to schedule in-service training for teachers. As mentioned earlier, interactional thinking and behavior are not necessarily easy for educators to accept and learn. While much learning takes place in CTI meetings, formal instruction, role play, and informal candid clinical discussion are also important. A weekly clinical case conference, in which collaboration cases are discussed, is one possible training format. The use of in-service training can be the difference in the success or failure of an ecosystemic collaborative program. The long-range answer to collaborative skill training for school personnel is curricular offerings at the undergraduate and graduate level and hands-on training during practicum assignments.

Seventh, ways need to be found to change the allocation procedures in school budgets. Efforts should be made early to engage the support of the superintendent of schools in finding ways to fund the program using existing sources of money. Funding may also be sought outside a particular school system through existing public or private grants of foundations or through private corporations. Businesses are spending substantial percentages of their budgets on retraining high school "graduates" in basic skills. Chrysler spends 11 percent of its total budget in this manner. Businesses like Nabisco are providing millions of dollars in school grants, which continue to be used primarily for such intrapsychic programs as individual mentoring, career education, and drug education. Some of this money can be redirected to interactional programs if school leaders will champion them.

A final implementation step is to maintain close and ongoing communication with the school decision makers. No matter how successful the program, there probably will be nay-sayers, who for various legitimate and other reasons, look for ways to denigrate the program. Maintaining a good relationship with school leaders is essential to the consultant's successful passage through the "mine fields."

Levels of Receptivity

The following two accounts of my efforts to establish collaboration programs in two school systems are given to provide concrete images of what lies ahead for proponents of school-based ecosystemic collaboration. In scenario A, although I worked diligently to identify a contact person in the school system, the school district remained closed to the idea even five years later. In scenario B, the school system opened up immediately.

Scenario A

In school system A, I spent several years contacting and meeting briefly with pupil personnel staff at the district high school and with central administration officials, including the superintendent of schools. I sent a great deal of material to these officials, including an earlier unpublished version of this book. I also gave a fifteen-minute presentation of the model to the district staff development committee. Three teachers in the district were highly satisfied clients in my private practice, but did not want to publicize that aspect of their private lives. During these five years, although my expertise as a therapist for children and families was well known, I received no referrals to my private practice from this entire school system and no invitations to speak, even for free, on any aspect of my work.

Starting in the fall of 1991, a resident of this particular town, who was a mother of two recent graduates of this school system's high school, began to agitate for the acceptance of the ecosystemic collaboration model. This mother had seen installments of my television show, "Parenting by Automatic Pilot," and had come to me for therapy and advice on how to manage her undermotivated and depressed eighteen-year-old. Although this mother had been in therapy before and had talked for years to school counselors and teachers, she still didn't clearly understand how to be a good parent. After seeing this writer's television show one time and after coming for one session of therapy, this mother volunteered her amazement at the simplicity of the principles. Coincidentally, at about this same time, this client's neighbor's son was one of four boys who died in her town from drug overdose and various accidents. The client had been aware of the problems in the boy's family and had recommended that her neighbor come to me for family counseling. The neighbor had procrastinated. Her son died about two weeks later.

After learning quickly how to parent and while in the process of recovering from the tragedy next door, my client began to approach several dozen education, government, religious, and other officials in her town with the concept of school collaboration for families. Everyone she spoke with was polite, but nothing happened. Not one official of dozens who were called was willing to investigate this idea. The client arranged for me to give four talks on parenting at a conference center in a neighboring town. These talks were well publicized in the client's town newspaper. Some school officials, the town mayor, and dozens of parents attended. Several parents sought me out for family therapy afterward, but still, not one school or municipal official would meet with me. Several of my clients, including the three teachers in the school system, did speak enthusiastically of my work at this time, but still, no response.

The client who had first made an effort on behalf of the collaboration program managed to have it included on the agenda for the school district's administrative council meeting. At the meeting I presented a federal grant application proposal that I had prepared that, if accepted, would have brought $50,000 to $200,000 into the school district. A complimentary personal letter from an official of the U.S. Department of Education accompanied the proposal. Lack of money had been used previously as a pseudoreason for the school's lack of interest in the program. This time no one in the school system was interested in the proposal. The idea of school-based ecosystemic collaboration was rejected.

After hundreds of hours of work by this writer over many years and after hundreds of hours by a client over several months, there is still no sign of acceptance of school-based ecosystems collaboration in this town and school district.

Scenario B

The presentation of school-based collaboration does not have to be as discouraging as it was in the first scenario. In school district B, my experience was quite different. The difference was not with the messenger, however, but with the receptivity of the school system to the message.

The pupil personnel director in school district B responded favorably to the first mailing of collaboration materials to his district. He set up a meeting of thirty staff people, including representatives from pupil personnel, administration, special education, and other constituencies. The staff liked what they heard, and I was invited back the following autumn for a one-day, six-hour in-service training program for ten staff members. Again, the staff were impressed. Six months later, I was asked to conduct my first ecosystems collaboration session in the school district's elementary school. Seventeen people attended the collaborative team intervention. It was extremely successful. Two days later, I was invited back to work with a second family, and within two or three months, there were several more referrals.

The preceding two vignettes have been presented to give contrasting examples of the openness of school systems to ecosystems collaboration. In scenario A, hundreds of hours by the consultant, hundreds of hours by a sympathetic town resident and mother of town school children, and many testimonials by satisfied clients made no dent in a district rigidly bound in intrapsychic, neuroedumedical concepts. In scenario B, a packet of information, a few phone calls, and a two-hour presentation opened the doors wide to a concept that made sense to the officials of another very different institution.

Seeing the School and Community as Family Systems

Whatever procedures are outlined for establishing or implementing an ecosystems collaboration program, the greatest effect will come from the application of family systems principles to the operation of the school and community themselves. Schools and communities are larger systems than families, but they are similar in having hierarchies, rules, and problems. In ecosystems collaboration sessions in school, personal problems of teachers, their bad attitudes toward children, their resentment toward principals, and personal teacher-teacher conflicts come to light. Great benefit can accrue to these larger systems if the managers of these systems—for example, superintendents of schools and mayors—are willing to look in the mirror themselves to analyze the way they manage or interact with their "children," namely, the educators and other employees in their "families." The personal characteristics of the relationships between the superintendent of schools and his principals, between the principals and their teachers, between the chief of police and his officers, and other such relationships will have a major impact on how teachers and children, teachers and parents, and parents and children relate to each other. When leaders of communities, schools, and other institutions use the dysfunctional management styles of overcontrol, undercontrol, overprotection, and underprotection, the employees will become "brats," "victims," "sociopaths," and "self-destroyers."

The prospective collaborationist is encouraged to offer intensive "family" weekends for various subsystems of the school and community. In these weekends, administrators, whole school staffs of specific buildings, or groups of community leaders can meet to analyze the way their system works. Points of view, conflicts, and complaints can be aired, as well as recommendations for solutions. These "family" weekends are, in effect, collaboration sessions for a school building staff, a police department, or a community partnership for children. The meetings are not "gripe" sessions, but solution-oriented meetings for communication, goal-setting, and conflict resolution. Dysfunctional personal and relationship issues are the greatest obstacles to the establishment of ecosystems collaboration programs in schools.

Unless school and community leaders are willing to ask their "families" to look in the mirror and change, teachers and other employees will not fully understand the connection between child problems and adult problems, and will continue to leave the resolution of child problems to specialists, that is, to anyone but themselves. Although the collaborative approach is principally focused on changing children, a side effect is that school and community institutions involved in collaboration also begin to change. It is in the wake of such large-scale institutional change that child problems can be most efficiently avoided or solved.

Summary

There are many obstacles to the acceptance and continued success of ecosystemic collaborative efforts in schools—but there are also many benefits to be gained from the use of this approach. To establish collaborative programs in schools, those interested in this approach must have more than excellent therapeutic skills. They must have unusual personal qualities of endurance and must be capable of securing the strong support of school officials who are real leaders. Attention to the "mine fields" in schools and use of the suggestions given in this chapter will provide these therapists and consultants with at least a rough map and guidelines that will be helpful to their mission.

12

FROM PILOT PROJECTS
TO STANDARD PRACTICES

Within the marriage and family therapy community, it is axiomatic that children are best understood and treated within the context of the systems in which they live, primarily the family, school, and community systems. Although conceptually, systems work with children was always meant to include all these systems, most of this work has focused on the families, without a clear integration with the other systems. More recent efforts in family therapy have dealt with an analysis of the family-school relationship and with ways in which systems concepts might be more integrated into school practice. I have identified and suggested several methods or models for involving schools in child problem solution, including systems-oriented case consultation in schools, in-service systems training for school personnel, training of school staff in how to make systems referrals, and hot-line telephone consultation for school staff.

In this book, I have argued for the importance of establishing ecosystems collaboration programs in schools. My argument has been based both on the desperate status of children in our society and on the effectiveness of the school-based ecosystems collaboration model. I have described the key components of the model and shown how it works through case examples. And I have provided suggestions for establishing the model in schools. In this final chapter, I want to summarize and analyze how the use of the model may affect children, families, schools, and communities and also consider the implications of the model for the practice of marriage and family therapy.

Impact on Children and Families

Children and families can continue to benefit from a family systems approach that is practiced selectively in mental health clinics and private offices, and in primary social institutions such as schools and courts. But while individual families are helped to "recover" from problems they already have, social institutions continue to participate in creating them. National statistics on school failure and dropout, crime, drug abuse, and other factors seem to indicate that we, as a society, are losing the battle and are in essence "shoveling sand against the tide."

The school-based ecosystems collaboration model arranges for the incorporation of the powerful tools of systems assessment and treatment into everyday school practice. The school is the logical site for this kind of program because children spend so much of their life there (approximately 50 percent of waking hours for 180 days a year), and because there exists in schools an "army" of trained professionals who, for the most part, care about and understand children. Many case studies have been presented in this book which detail the use of the school-based ecosystems collaboration model and which I hope illustrate for the reader ways in which it differs from current school-related or school-linked services. The advantages for children and families that proceed from the use of the school-based ecosystems collaborative model appear to include the following:

1. There is an increased ability in the collaborative model described in this book for assessment and treatment of child problems to be ecosystemic. School personnel still tend to follow an individual, intrapsychic model of assessment and intervention that

emphasizes the diagnostic layaway plan of testing, individual counseling, disorder labeling, and special placements. The collaborative model calls for the training of all school staff in ecosystemic ideas and the use of this training in direct interaction with parents and others about causes of child problems that relate to parent-child relationships, marital problems, teacher-parent conflict, and other relationship issues. It also provides for the direct on-site processing of these issues with all parties involved. Current school and social practice generally follows a nonintegrated, specialized referral model, which involves teachers referring family matters to specialists in school, and schools referring these matters out of school. Dealing with family and other interactional problems in school, with everyone involved taking ownership of the problem, increases the accuracy of ecosystemic analysis and the effectiveness of ecosystemic treatment.

2. With this model problems are identified earlier. As stated above, teachers are asked to play more ecosystemically sophisticated and active roles. When children's problems do not respond to individual motivational or other pedagogical techniques, teachers do not wait weeks or months to ask for help, and when they do ask, it is for ecosystemic help. The chances are great in this model that child problems will be detected early.

3. The availability of a school-based model increases the likelihood of engaging families in problem-solving efforts. Many authors have noted the difficulty of engaging families in treatment settings outside the school. The proximity of the school, parent familiarity with its physical characteristics, general parent trust in school personnel, the absence of financial cost for the service, and other factors make it more likely that parents will accept service in school more than a referral to a setting outside of school.

4. It is important to stress the low-stigmatizing nature of the model. Although family issues are raised, including sensitive marital issues, the helpful character of school efforts and the presence of many people in larger meetings helps to normalize the discussion and reframe the problems that seem extreme as normal. A structured flip chart and chalkboard systemic analysis of parent-child and adult issues allows parents and children to view their problems more objectively and dispassionately as examples of be-

havior in a larger human context. Conducting family therapy in this large, nonconfidential, public context often paradoxically increases comfort level and reduces resistance to new ideas.

5.   The collaborative model multiplies the number of helpers and types of interactions that can occur between family members and school personnel and others. When child and family problems are jobs for various specialists who focus on restricted types of problems, the range of discussion is also restricted. When all matters are everyone's business, more help is potentially forthcoming. Parents who have mentioned marital or financial problems to teachers or other educators usually feel freer to continue discussions of these matters during informal encounters.

6.   Through the collaborative model, the destructive features of rules of privacy and confidentiality are reduced or eliminated. Whereas in the models currently in use, one can scarcely get through a sentence without apologizing for the inability to be frank because of confidentiality, the school-based ecosystems collaborative model provides for all relevant players to be involved in open communication.

7.   In the collaborative approach, children are included more often in meetings about them and are given more credit for the ability to solve their own problems or participate in a solution. They are really treated like equals in collaborative efforts, even when their unwillingness to cooperate results in hierarchical measures being taken to control them.

8.   The ability of children to help themselves is increased. When child, family, and school issues have been discussed in public in school, children generally feel more empowered to conduct their own self-therapy in the form of more assertive conversations with family members and with teachers, other school adults, and other children in school or in the neighborhood. When services are provided outside of school, there is generally a greater need to respect boundaries and keep secrets.

9.   In school-based ecosystems collaboration, problems of all family members, including children in different schools in a school district, can be treated at the same time. Current efforts tend to be handled on a school-by-school basis. When all children in a

family attend the same meeting, the likelihood of more comprehensive family and general ecological restructuring is enhanced.

10. Finally, through the increased openness of communication fostered by this model, interfamily communication and mutual help in the neighborhood and community is fostered. Family members imbued with a low-stigmatizing frame around their problem are more likely to initiate and respond to conversations with friends, acquaintances, and extended family that focus on important areas of life that were formerly too sensitized to discuss.

The benefits to children and families from an open, school-based model of problem-solving that is ecosystemic and collaborative are many. An effort has been made to detail some of them in this book. The reader is left to judge the potential advantages of the collaborative model in relation to current approaches to services for children and families.

Impact on the School

In addition to its influence on children and families, ecosystemic collaboration has direct and indirect effects on school structure and function. In the first collaborative session with the first child referred to an ecosystemic collaboration program, teachers begin to hear more about the family—information they usually have not heard before, for example, that the child's father was just like the child at this age, or that the mother and father disagree vehemently about how the child should behave. Witnessing these revelations helps teachers and others to abandon their intrapsychic focus on the individual behavior of the child and to redirect their thinking to the interactional factors that are the primary causes of child behavior.

Another effect of collaborative activity is that teachers and other educators can learn how to work with families on difficult family issues. Teachers often report being at first rattled and uncomfortable in these situations, but they are asked to stay, and they hear and see things they would tend not to ask about and would generally avoid in one-to-one interactions with parents. (When mothers begin to cry, for example, a frequent occurrence at collaborative meetings, teachers tend to comfort the mothers and move away from the topic that caused the stress. After hearing of the father's abusive behavior toward a child, for example, teachers would probably not want to meet him or deal with him.) Teachers are supported in these cases by the presence of several school personnel, often including an administrator, who help to make the situation more manageable.

A key to the initial success of ecosystemic collaboration is that an ecosystems expert—someone outside the school, or someone internal to the school, for example, the school psychologist—is conducting the meeting. The teacher can initially concentrate on giving information and can leave the confrontation or negotiation with parents primarily to the consultant. Teachers who have been ill-trained in dealing intimately with parents can learn how to communicate ecosystemically at close range, in a purposeful, personal way. Teachers can watch parent-child interactions orchestrated by the consultant and consider the similarities and differences in their own interactions with a child. A child's behavior, heretofore mysterious and/or infuriating, can become more understandable when seen in conjunction with parental behavior. When teachers observe the undercontrolling, overprotective behavior of a mother, they may temporarily shift their anger from the child to the mother. Causes of the child's behavior can then be addressed.

Because of the intimacy established in collaborative sessions, teachers and school personnel can begin to see the pain and desperation parents are experiencing and can henceforth relate to them on a different level. Interpersonal barriers are often discarded by both parents and school personnel under the pressure of group efforts to solve a child's problem. Few child problems can continue in the context of this intimate, honest relating between intelligent, caring adults. The teachers of a "terrorist" child can learn to sympathize with the mother when they actually meet and talk with her. When educators observe these processes in action, they often want to get more involved.

Another effect of collaboration is that educators begin to make solving the child's problem a top priority. The collaborative session results in a team plan for child success. Procrastination, discouragement, and other negative attitudes lose their power to interfere with success. School personnel begin to treat other child problems in the same way and to believe that all child problems can be solved instead of "lived with." It has unfortunately been the case that despite increasing official rhetoric about team planning in schools, many teachers have still tried to solve problems by themselves. They have considered it a personal failure when a child does not succeed. Collaboration sessions model a "team" intervention, and team interactions tend to continue after the formal sessions.

Finally, as a result of collaboration sessions, teacher-teacher and other school staff interactions begin to take on a different flavor. Formal interactions, for example, child study team or PPT meetings, become solution-oriented and influenced by systems thinking. Informal interactions begin to be more positive and full of child success stories, instead of weather, gossip, or complaints about this or that "impossible" child. Most teachers do not enjoy swapping discouraging stories about children. They simply feel frustrated and helpless and want to vent their feelings. The provision of a vehicle for success tends to produce a spontaneous positive shift in the flavor and content of staff interactions. Interdisciplinary staff interactions tend to become more intimate, and the barriers begin to drop between administrators and teachers and between regular teachers and special teachers. Personal revelations by school staff to parents are now public knowledge for use by school staff with each other. A school's climate can be positively affected when school staff are somewhat open about their personal lives. School staff can apply to their own lives some of the ideas and techniques they learn in collaborative sessions. They can benefit as parents and marriage partners, as well as in their professional and educational roles. In several instances, teachers have initiated personal therapy with me following experiences in collaborative sessions.

The impact of ecosystemic collaboration on school climate is probably its greatest benefit. Educators have great influence over children, second only to parents. Adoption of the ecosystemic collaborative philosophy leads to a commitment by a school staff to the prompt solution of all significant child problems and to a greater commitment to continued use of the ecosystems collaboration model.

Impact on the Community

Just as collaborative work in schools begins to affect the school environment, so does it begin to affect the structure of the community in several ways. Parents begin to talk to other parents more frequently about systems, metaphors, and families of origin. Child problems are increasingly seen by all as symptoms of adult and societal problems. Many parents new to the collaborative program are referred to other parents who have successfully changed their interactions with their children and/or school staff. A kind of informal parent network begins to develop in the community. Adults hearing about collaboration begin to blame kids less and take more responsibility in the community for leading the way. These adults begin to "look in the mirror" and shift the focus of their efforts from their children to themselves—to their own individual and marital problems.

A second community effect of the use of ecosystemic collaboration is that parents not involved in collaboration begin to approach the school more assertively and with the hope of more constructive interaction with school staff. They are more willing to be honest about personal, private matters because of a new image of openness created by the school. Referrals to the collaboration program begin to be initiated by parents as well as by school staff.

A third effect of the use of ecosystemic collaboration is that parents are less likely to label children and send them to special education, rehabilitation centers, and hospitals. Changing their home life is seen as a better alternative. This development is very important. For years parents have not known of solutions to child problems available in their own communities. They have been advised by many professionals and groups to use the hospital or residential alternative. Parents who have followed this course of action find it very difficult to recover from the guilt they feel. They know deep down that it was unnecessary and/or destructive. Now they have an alternative. "Special" programs in communities begin to focus more attention on changing family life instead of ignoring parents or taking their children away from them. Family meetings become an integral component of Drug Abuse Resistance Education (DARE) or Here's Looking at You 2000 programs, community teen centers, and judicial and hospital procedures.

A fourth effect of the use of ecosystemic collaboration is that taxpayers and boards of education begin to realize that it is a lot cheaper to pay for a few collaboration sessions than to send children to special schools, or hospitals, or rehabilitation centers. Schools have at times spent $100,000 or more a year on these programs for one child. Special priorities and patterns begin to shift in the direction of prevention and away from rehabilitation, and interaction with families becomes a major focus of community spending.

A fifth effect is on the functioning of service agencies. Private medical doctors and therapists begin to revise their diagnoses and treatments from individually based to systems-based, and to be more attentive to the need to communicate with schools. Diagnoses of attention deficit, learning disability, childhood depression, and allergy become less frequent as the medical and mental health professions are educated in the powerful effects of the child's system. Medications are used less, as their uselessness or destructive side-effects become more obvious. Police forces, judicial systems, and hospitals become more systems conscious, and personnel in these institutions put more time and resources into discussions of adult dynamics and less into treatment and punishment of individual children.

A sixth effect is that the notion of privacy or confidentiality is radically revised since all the relevant players are now defined as part of the problem and part of the solution. When most of the people involved with a child are in the same room in a collaboration session, everyone becomes aware of the story. The need for privacy is thereby eliminated or reduced. A free flow of communication among all relevant parties is facilitated, and collaboration begins to be less a discrete school activity and more a way of life in the community.

Implications for National Leadership in the Helping Professions

Larger system thinking and, specifically, the theory and practice of school-based ecosystems collaboration, has several potential implications for the functioning of the individual marriage and family therapist, psychologist, and other therapist, as well as for the leadership of such professional associations as the American Association for Marriage and Family Therapy, the American Psychological

Association, and other organizations. They are summarized as follows:

First, acceptance of the preferability of an ecosystems versus systems approach involves a shift in focus and practice to greater consideration of factors that are external to the family but that nevertheless affect it. From this perspective, the behavior of school personnel, youth officers, court officers, judges, and medical doctors becomes more relevant to the therapist, and he or she may seek to become more of an active player in larger system dynamics. A family therapist may want to arrange interviews with the director and staff of a psychiatric unit, probation department, or department of youth services in an attempt to influence them and work with them in the adoption of more systems-oriented policies, for example, the use of family therapy instead of incarceration or residential addiction treatment. The ecosystemic therapist/consultant would be inclined to be much more interested in positively affecting the family-school relationship and in facilitating the school adoption of an ecosystemic perspective.

Second, acceptance of the ecosystemic collaborative concept defines the therapist as one of a group of collaborators who work together, rather than as an expert working alone on one aspect of the larger system, namely, the family. For private or clinic practitioners, practice of the collaborative philosophy could potentially involve more telephone calls or meetings in or out of the office with professionals who were heretofore defined as referral sources. Family therapists working in school would become ecosystems therapists who widen the loop of interaction assessment and intervention. Further, in a collaborative context in a school, the family is an equal collaborator as well as a therapeutic client. Therapist behavior may have to change under the assumptions of a collaborative role in a school, which is different from the traditional therapist role of confidential expert. For example, family therapists operating in collaboratively oriented schools will sometimes be asked for opinions in public meetings that normally they would not reveal to their clients. In this context, there is a greater pressure on the therapist to explain problems in a way that is acceptable to multiple constituencies, not just the family.

Third, if mental health and other services are going to be

based more in schools, the family therapist may wish to be involved in providing school-based services rather than being only a receiver of school referrals. He or she may, in addition, want to lead the way in introducing such ideas to schools, providing in-service staff training in ecosystems collaboration, and consulting with school systems in the development of school-based programs. Private practitioners with a school-based focus would very likely refer many of their private cases to collaboration programs in schools to facilitate the activation of school-based teams, because they multiply and diversify the number of helpers for children with school or home problems. These practitioners would probably spend relatively much more of their professional lives in schools and in consultation with school-based or other professionals involved in collaborative interventions.

There may also be some implications for the professional leadership in the American Association for Marriage and Family Therapy and other state and national associations. A great deal of effort and money has been expended over recent years in educating the public, government officials, and insurance carriers in the value of systems assessment and interventions. Association recommendations to these officials and organizations may shift from support of private and separate family work to greater focus on institutional adoption of programs based on larger system thinking. Government officials besieged by political action committees may be intrigued by the thought of a model in which many constituencies are involved together in one united effort and where all varieties of problems can be treated. Current funding practices seem most frequently to involve separate, competitive funding for problems like drug addiction, crime, and school failure, which are considered disconnected problems. Additional association efforts could be directed at state certification and insurance procedures to clear the way for schools to hire family therapists and for schools to receive insurance compensation for collaborative services in schools. Finally, the national and state associations can recommend the development of courses or concentrations in school-based ecosystems collaboration for use in marriage and family training programs and the incorporation of these courses in clinical and supervisory certification requirements.

In the End, a Question of Leadership

When all is said and done, the future of school-based ecosystems collaboration ultimately hinges mainly on one factor, and that factor is leadership. As mentioned earlier, the true leader possesses an abundance of courage, caring, and wisdom. No matter how much information is gathered to support the ecosystemic collaboration concept, no matter how much training school staff are given, no matter how much funding is available for the program, it is the clear and consistent experience of this writer that nothing will make any difference without leadership. Politicians, school superintendents, presidents of professional associations, and others may be blessed with one or two of these qualities of leadership, but very few have all three.

For ecosystemic collaboration programs to succeed, a leader must be identified, someone who cares deeply about the welfare of children, who clearly understands and believes in the value of the use of the ecosystems collaboration approach, and who has the fortitude to resist and overcome the barrage of criticism that will often accompany the introduction and continued use of this model. The highest priority for those interested in establishing collaboration programs must be to identify, encourage, pester, and work with these leaders until they develop the necessary level of commitment to the program.

The school-based ecosystems collaborative movement is unfortunately still in its infancy. Although recommendations for ecological intervention have been available for a quarter of a century, and although hundreds of articles have been published on the topic of family-school intervention, ecosystems collaboration in schools is still considered a pilot project. The rather slow-motioned acceptance of the ecosystems collaborative model is a testimony to general societal resistance to any change, but also perhaps to a special resistance of family, school, and community systems to the controversial nature of this concept. In any case, proponents of this model must be ready for resistance to and even rejection of their efforts to have this model accepted.

I believe that school-based ecosystems collaboration is necessary for the success of family and school functioning in the 1990s and in the twenty-first century. Children will continue to abuse and be abused until we begin to emphasize work with their families and other systems. Every child alive has at least one adult who loves it or one who can be found to love it. That adult is its "family." If we change our focus to the families and ecosystems of children, we can change children, usually without punishment and without tiresome and expensive bureaucratic procedures. Children do not belong in school detention, on school suspension, in jails, or in rehabilitation centers. These measures are largely unnecessary if families and other systems are helped to manage children. Intrapsychic thinking and the disorders of control and protection by adults embedded in dysfunctional interactional patterns have created a crisis situation. Examples of child problems and ecosystemic, school-based, collaborative solutions have been provided in this book in the hope of stimulating a switch in thinking and practice from the intrapsychic mode to the interactional. Adherence to our current policy of either blaming or excusing the child and ignoring those who trained the child will only perpetuate the present crisis in child misbehavior, underachievement, and unhappiness.

For half the year, children spend 50 percent of their waking hours under the supervision of teachers and other school support staff. The school is the ideal place for collaborative work between educators, community workers, and children's first and primary teachers—their parents. Unfortunately, at the present time, very few school, business, or government officials envision or accept the role of facilitating the establishment of school-based ecosystems collaborative programs. The failure to do so makes their jobs more difficult and deprives children and parents of a crucial ingredient in their ability to cope and change. What is needed in schools is a collaborative format in which teachers and other school personnel approach, or are approached by, parents in honest and candid ways, and in which real individual or marital issues are discussed, including parenting disagreements, individual issues of anxiety and depression, marital conflicts, family-of-origin problems, and other issues. School problems need to be frankly admitted by school personnel, and joint strategies need to be devised to solve the problems without blaming the children. Adults need to be given change assignments, releasing children to resume their privileges and responsibilities.

With persevering emphasis on the philosophy and procedures outlined in this book, it is hoped that members of the helping professions can facilitate the reclassification of school-based ecosystems collaboration from pilot project to standard practice and national priority. Perhaps, some day, "collaborative team intervention" will be just as much a household expression as detention, learning disability, and PPT.

References

Alexander, F., and French, T. *Psychoanalytic Therapy*. New York: Ronald, 1946.

Alexander, J. F., Barton, C., Schiavo, R. G., and Parsons, B. V. "Systems-Behavioral Intervention with Families of Delinquents: Therapist Characteristics, Family Behavior, and Outcome." *Journal of Consulting and Clinical Psychology*, 1976, *44*(4), 656-664.

Alexander, J., and Parsons, B. "Short-Term Behavioral Intervention with Delinquent Families: Impact on Family Process and Recidivism." *Journal of Abnormal Psychology*, 1973, *81*(3), 219-225.

Amatea, E. S., and Fabrick, F. "Family Systems Counseling: A Positive Alternative to Traditional Counseling." *Elementary School Guidance and Counseling*, 1981, *15*(3), 223-236.

Amatea, E. S., and Fabrick, F. "Moving a Family into Therapy: Critical Referral Issues for the School Counselor." *School Counselor*, Jan. 1984, pp. 285-294.

Anderson, C. "An Ecological Development Model for a Family Orientation in School Psychology." *Journal of School Psychology*, 1983, *21*, 179–189.

Andolfi, M. *Family Therapy: An International Approach*. London: Plenum, 1979.

Andolfi, M., Angelo, C., Menghi, P., and Nicolo-Corigliano, A. M. *Behind the Family Mask*. New York: Brunner/Mazel, 1983.

Andolfi, M., Stein, D. D., and Skinner, J. "A Systems Approach to the Child, School, Family and Community in an Urban Area." *American Journal of Community Psychology*, 1977, *5*(1), 33–43.

Aponte, H. J. "The Family-School Interview: An Eco-Structural Approach." *Family Process*, 1976, *15*, 303–312.

Apter, S. J. *Troubled Children: Troubled Systems*. Elmsford, N.Y.: Pergamon Press, 1982.

Atkenson, B. M., and Forehand, R. "Parent Behavioral Training: An Examination of Studies Using Multiple Outcome Measures." *Journal of Abnormal Child Psychology*, 1978, *6*, 449–460.

Auerswald, E. "Interdisciplinary Versus Ecological Approach." *Family Process*, 1968, *17*, 202–215.

Baker, F. "Custodians Give Speech with a Twist at N.H. Rite." *Boston Globe*, Jun. 16, 1991.

Bandura, A. *Principles of Behavior Modification*. New York: Holt, Rinehart & Winston, 1969.

Bandura, A. "Self-Efficacy: Toward a Unifying Theory of Behavioral Change." *Psychological Review*, 1977, *84*, 191–215.

Barker, R. G. "Explorations in Ecological Psychology." *American Psychologist*, 1965, *20*, 1–14.

Barkley, R. A. "Hyperactivity." In E. J. Mash and L. G. Terdal (eds.), *Behavioral Assessment of Childhood Disorders*. New York: Guilford, 1981.

Bateson, G. *Steps to an Ecology of Mind*. New York: Ballantine Books, 1972.

Bergan, J. R. *Behavioral Consultation*. Columbus, Ohio: Merrill, 1977.

Berger, S. R., Shoul, R., and Warschauer, S. "A School-Based Divorce Intervention Program." In M. J. Fine and C. Carlson (eds.), *Handbook of Family-School Intervention: A Systems Perspective*. Boston: Allyn & Bacon, 1992.

Berkowitz, B. P., and Graziano, A. M. "Training Parents as Behavior Therapists: A Review." *Behavior Research and Therapy,* 1972, *10,* 297–317.

Bowen, M. *Family Therapy in Clinical Practice.* New York: Jason Aronson, 1978.

Braden, J. P., and Sherrard, P.A.D. "Referring Families to Nonschool Agencies: A Family Systems Approach." *School Psychology Review,* 1987, *16*(4), 513–518.

Brickman, P., and others. "Models of Helping and Coping." *American Psychologist,* 1982, *37,* 368–384.

Bronfenbrenner, U. *The Ecology of Human Development: Experiments by Nature and Design.* Cambridge, Mass.: Harvard University Press, 1979.

Caplan, G. *The Theory and Practice of Mental Health Consultation.* New York: Basic Books, 1970.

Carkhuff, R. R. *Helping and Human Relations: A Primer for Lay and Professional Helpers.* Vols. I and II. New York: Holt, Rinehart & Winston, 1969.

Carl, D., and Jurkovic, G. J., "Agency Triangles: Problems in Agency-Family Relationships." *Family Process,* 1983, *22*(12), 441–451.

Carlson, C. I. "Models and Strategies of Family-School Assessment and Intervention." In M. J. Fine and C. Carlson (eds.), *Handbook of Family-School Intervention: A Systems Perspective.* Boston: Allyn & Bacon, 1992.

Carlson, C. I. "Resolving School Problems with Structural Family Therapy." *School Psychology Review,* 1987, *16*(4), 457–468.

Carlson, C. I., and Sincavage, J. M. "Family-Oriented School Psychology Practice: Results of a National Survey of NASP Members." *School Psychology Review,* 1987, *16*(4), 519–526.

Cohen, S., and Syme, L. (eds.). *Social Support and Health.* New York: Academic Press, 1985.

Coleman, J. S. "Families and Schools." *Educational Researcher,* 1987, *16*(6), 32–38.

Compher, J. V. "Parent-School-Child Systems: Triadic Assessment and Intervention." *Social Casework: The Journal of Contemporary Social Work,* Sept. 1982, pp. 415–423.

Cone, J. D., and Sloop, E. W. "Parents as Agents of Change." In

A. Jacobs and W. W. Spradlin (eds.), *Group as Agent of Change.* Chicago: Aldine-Atherton, 1971.

Conoley, J. "Strategic Family Intervention: Three Cases of School-Aged Children." *School-Psychology Review,* 1987, *16*(4), 469-486.

Conti, A. P. "A Follow-Up Study of Families Referred to Outside Agencies." *Psychology in the Schools,* 1971, *8,* 338-340.

Conti, A. P. "A Follow-Up Investigation of Families Referred to Outside Agencies." *Journal of School Psychology,* 1973, *11,* 215-222.

Conti, A. P. "Variables Related to Contacting/Not Contacting Counseling Services Recommended by School Psychologists." *Journal of School Psychology,* 1975, *13,* 41-50.

Crnic, K., Friedrich, W., and Greenberg, M. "Adaptation of Families with Mentally Retarded Children: A Model of Stress, Coping, and Family Ecology." *American Journal of Mental Deficiency,* 1983, *88,* 125-138.

DePaulo, B., Nadler, A., and Fisher, J. (eds.). *New Directions in Helping.* Vol. 2: *Helpseeking.* New York: Academic Press, 1983.

de Shazer, S. *Patterns of Brief Family Therapy: An Ecosystemic Approach.* New York: Guilford Press, 1982.

de Shazer, S. *Keys to Solution in Brief Therapy.* New York: Norton, 1985.

DiCocco, B. E. "A Guide to Family/School Interventions for the Family Therapist." *Contemporary Family Therapy,* 1986, *8,* 50-61.

DiCocco, B., and Lott, E. "Family/School Strategies in Dealing with the Troubled Child." *International Journal of Family Therapy,* 1982, *4*(2), 98-106.

Dinkmeyer, D., and McKay, G. *Systemic Training for Effective Parenting.* Circle Pines, Minn.: American Guidance Services, 1976.

Dombalis, A. O., and Erchul, W. P. "Multiple Family Group Therapy: A Review of Its Applicability to the Practice of School Psychology." *School Psychology Review,* 1987, *16*(4), 487-497.

Dreikurs, R. "Emotional Predisposition to Reading Difficulties." *Archives of Pediatrics,* 1954, *71*(11), 339-353.

Dreikurs, R., and Soltz, V. *Children: The Challenge.* New York: Meredith Press, 1964.

Dunst, C. J., and Trivette, C. M. "Enabling and Empowering Families: Conceptual and Intervention Issues." *School Psychology Review*, 1987, *16*(4), 443–456.

Ehrlich, M. F. "Psychofamial Correlates of School Disorders." *Journal of School Psychology*, 1983, *21*, 191–199.

Elizur, J., and Minuchin, S. *Institutionalizing Madness: Families, Therapy, and Society*. New York: Basic Books, 1989.

Eno, M. M. "Children with School Problems: A Family Therapy Perspective." In R. Ziffer (ed.), *Adjunctive Techniques of Family Therapy*. Orlando, Fla.: Grune & Stratton, 1985.

Erchul, W. P., and Conoley, C. W. "Helpful Theories to Guide Counselors' Practice of School-Based Consultation." *Elementary School Guidance and Counseling*, 1991, *25*, 204–211.

Fabrick, F., and Wagner, M. "The Story of T.J.: A Closer Look at School/Agency Cooperation." *Elementary School Guidance and Counseling*, 1981, *15*, 188–194.

Fine, M. J. "Integrating Structural and Strategic Components in School-Based Intervention: Some Cautions for Consultants." *Techniques*, 1984, *1*(1), 44–52.

Fine, M. J. "A Systems-Ecological Perspective on Home-School Intervention." In M. J. Fine and C. Carlson (eds.), *Handbook of Family-School Intervention: A Systems Perspective*. Boston: Allyn & Bacon, 1992.

Fine, M. J., and Holt, P. "Intervening with School Problems: A Family Systems Perspective." *Psychology in the Schools*, 1983, *20*(1), 59–66.

Fine, M. J., and Jennings, J. "What Parent Education Can Learn from Family Therapy." *Social Work in Education*, 1985, *8*(1), 14–30.

Fine, M. J., and Jennings, J. "Family Therapy's Contribution to Parent Education." In M. J. Fine and C. Carlson (eds.), *The Handbook of Family-School Intervention: A Systems Perspective*. Needham Heights, Mass.: Allyn & Bacon, 1992.

Fish, M. C., and Jain, S. "Using Systems Theory in School Assessment and Intervention: A Structural Model for School Psychologists." *Professional School Psychology*, 1988, *3*(4), 291–300.

Fisher, L. "Systems-Based Consultation with Schools." In L. C. Wynne, S. H. McDaniel, and T. T. Weber (eds.), *Systems Con-

sultation: A New Perspective for Family Therapy. New York: Guilford Press, 1986.

Foster, M. A. "Schools." In M. Berger and G. J. Jurkovic (eds.), *Practicing Family Therapy in Diverse Settings.* San Francisco: Jossey-Bass, 1984.

Freud, A. *Normality and Pathology in Childhood.* New York: International Universities Press, 1965.

Friedman, R. "A Structured Family Interview in the Assessment of School Learning Disorders." *Psychology in the Schools,* 1969, *6,* 162–171.

Friesen, J. "Family Counseling: A New Frontier for School Counseling." *Canadian Counsellor,* 1976, *10,* 180–184.

Gallessich, J. *The Profession and Practice of Consultation.* San Francisco: Jossey-Bass, 1982.

Gibbs, N. "Shameful Bequests to the Next Generation." *Time,* Oct. 8, 1990, pp. 42–47.

Ginott, H. *Between Parent and Child.* New York: Macmillan, 1965.

Ginott, H. *Between Parent and Teenager.* New York: Macmillan, 1969.

Golden, L. "Brief Family Interventions in a School Setting." *Elementary School Guidance and Counseling,* 1983, *17,* 288–293.

Goldenberg, I., and Goldenberg, H. "Family Systems and the School Counselor." *School Counselor,* 1981, *28,* 165–177.

Goodman, R. W., and Kjonaas, D. "Elementary School Family Counseling: A Pilot Project." *Journal of Counseling and Development,* 1984, *63,* 255–257.

Gordon, T. "Parent Effectiveness Training: A Preventive Program and Its Effects on Families." In M. Fine (ed.), *Handbook on Parent Education.* New York: Academic Press, 1980.

Green, B. J. "Systems Intervention in the Schools." In M. Mirken and S. Komar (eds.), *Handbook of Adolescent Therapy.* New York: Gardner, 1985.

Green, K., and Fine, M. J. "Family Therapy: A Case for Training for School Psychologists." *Psychology in the Schools,* 1980, *17,* 241–248.

Gurman, A., and Kniskern, D. "Research on Marital and Family Therapy: Progress, Perspective, and Prospect." In S. Garfield and A. Bergin (eds.), *Handbook of Psychotherapy and Behavior*

Change: An Empirical Analysis (2nd ed.). New York: Wiley, 1978.

Haley, J. *Problem-Solving Therapy* (2nd ed.). San Francisco: Jossey-Bass, 1987.

Henderson, A. T. *Evidence Continues to Grow: Parent Involvement Improves Student Achievement.* Columbia, Md.: National Committee for Citizens in Education, 1987.

Hobbs, N. "Helping Disturbed Children: Psychological and Ecological Strategies." *American Psychologist,* 1966, *21,* 1105–1115.

Hobbs, N. *The Futures of Children.* San Francisco: Jossey-Bass, 1975.

Hobbs, N., and others. *Strengthening Families.* San Francisco: Jossey-Bass, 1984.

Hoffmann, L., and Long, L. "A Systems Dilemma." *Family Process,* 1969, *8,* 211–234.

Imber-Black, E. *Families and Larger Systems.* New York: Guilford Press, 1988.

Jackson, D. D. "The Individual and the Larger Context." *Family Process,* 1967, *6*(2), 139–147.

Klein, N., Alexander, J., and Parsons, B. "Impact of Family Systems Intervention on Recidivism and Sibling Delinquency: A Model of Primary Prevention and Program Evolution." *Journal of Consulting and Clinical Psychology,* 1977, *45,* 469–474.

Knox, B. E. "Family Counseling: An In-Service Model." *School Counselor,* 1981, *28,* 202–206.

Kral, R. "Solution-focused Brief Therapy: Applications in the Schools." In M. J. Fine and C. Carlson (eds.), *Handbook of Family-School Intervention: A Systems Perspective.* Boston: Allyn & Bacon, 1992.

Kramer, J. "Family Counseling as a Key to Successful Alternative School Programs for Alienated Youth." *School Counselor,* 1977, *24,* 194–196.

Kuhn, T. *The Structure of Scientific Revolutions.* University of Chicago Press, 1970.

L'Abate, L., Baggett, M. S., and Anderson, J. S. "Linear and Circular Interventions with Families of Children with School-Related Problems." In J. Hansen and B. Okun (eds.), *Family*

Therapy with School Related Problems. Rockville, Md.: Aspen, 1984.

Lightfoot, S. L. *Worlds Apart: Relationships Between Families and Schools.* New York: Basic Books, 1978.

Lombard, T. J. "Family-Oriented Emphasis for School Psychologists: A Needed Orientation for Training and Practice." *Professional Psychology,* 1979, *10,* 687–696.

London, C. B., Molotsi, P. H., and Palmer, A. "Collaboration of Family, Community, and School in a Reconstructive Approach to Teaching and Learning." *Journal of Negro Education,* 1984, *53*(4), 455–463.

Loven, M. D. "Four Alternative Approaches to the Family/School Liaison Role." *Psychology in the Schools,* 1978, *15,* 553–559.

Lusterman, D. D. "An Ecosystemic Approach to Family-School Problems." *American Journal of Family Therapy,* 1985, *13*(1), 22–30.

Lusterman, D. D. "Ecosystemic Treatment of Family-School Problems: A Private Practice Perspective." In M. J. Fine and C. Carlson (eds.), *Handbook of Family-School Intervention: A Systems Perspective.* Boston: Allyn & Bacon, 1992.

McDaniel, S. H. "Treating School Problems in Family Therapy." *Elementary School Guidance and Counseling,* 1981, *15*(3), 214–222.

Martin, R. P. "Consultant, Consultee, and Client Expectations of Each Other's Behavior in Consultation." *School Psychology Review,* 1983, *12*(1), 35–41.

The Merriam-Webster Thesaurus. New York: Simon & Schuster, 1978.

Meyer, P. *Dynamics of Personal Goal Setting.* Waco, Tex.: Success Motivation Institute, 1984.

Miller, D. R., and Westman, J. C. "Reading Disability as a Condition of Family Stability." *Family Process,* 1964, *3,* 66–76.

Miller, W. B. "Inter-Institutional Conflict as a Major Impediment to Delinquency Prevention." *Human Organization,* 1974, *17,* 20–23.

Minard, S. "Family Systems Model in Organization Consultation." *Family Process,* 1976, *15,* 313–320.

Minor, M. W. "Systems Analysis and School Psychology." *Journal of School Psychology,* 1972, *10*(3), 227–232.

Minuchin, S. "The Use of an Ecological Framework in the Treatment of a Child." In E. J. Anthony and C. Koupernik (eds.), *International Yearbook of Child Psychiatry: The Child in His Family.* New York: Wiley, 1970.

Minuchin, S. *Families and Family Therapy.* Cambridge, Mass.: Harvard University Press, 1974.

Newman, R. *Psychological Consultation in the Schools.* New York: Basic Books, 1967.

Nicoll, W. "School Counselors as Family Counselors: A Rationale and Training Model." *School Counselor,* 1984, *31*(3), 279–284.

O'Dell, S. "Training Parents in Behavior Modification: A Review." *Psychological Bulletin,* 1974, *81,* 418–433.

Okun, B. F. "Family Therapy and the Schools." In J. C. Hansen and B. Okun (eds.), *Family Therapy with School-Related Problems.* Rockville, Md.: Aspen Systems, 1984.

Paget, K. "Systemic Family Assessment: Concepts and Strategies for School Psychologists." *School Psychology Review,* 1987, *16*(4), 429–442.

Palmo, A. J., Lowry, L. A., Weldon, D. P., and Scoscia, T. M. "Schools and Family: Future Perspectives for School Counselors." *School Counselor,* 1984, *31*(3), 272–278.

Patterson, G. R. *Families: Application of Social Learning to Family Life.* Champaign, Ill.: Research Press, 1971.

Patterson, G. R., and Brodsky, G. D. "A Behavior Modification Program for a Child with Multiple Behavior Problems." *Journal of Child Psychology and Psychiatry,* 1966, *7,* 277–295.

Patterson, G. R., DeBarsyske, B. D., and Ramsey, E. "A Developmental Perspective on Antisocial Behavior." *American Psychologist,* 1989, *44,* 329–335.

Patterson, G. R., and Gullion, E. M. *Living with Children: New Methods for Parents and Teachers.* Champaign, Ill.: Research Press, 1971.

Peele, S. *Diseasing of America.* Lexington, Mass.: Lexington Books, 1989.

Perosa, L. M., and Perosa, S. L., "The School Counselor's Use of

Structural Family Therapy with Learning Disabled Students."
School Counselor, 1981, *29,* 152–155.

Pfeiffer, S. I., and Tittler, B. I. "Utilizing the Multidisciplinary
Team to Facilitate a School-Family Systems Orientation."
School Psychology Review, 1983, *12,* 168–173.

Plas, J. M. *Systems Psychology in the Schools.* Elmsford, N.Y.:
Pergamon Press, 1986.

Plas, J. M. "The Development of Systems Thinking: A Historical
Perspective." In M. J. Fine and C. Carlson (eds.), *Handbook of
Family-School Intervention: A Systems Perspective.* Boston: Al-
lyn & Bacon, 1992.

Power, T. J., and Bartholomew, K. L. "Getting Uncaught in the
Middle: A Case Study in Family-School System Consultation."
School Psychology Review, 1985, *14*(2), 222–229.

Power, T. J., and Bartholomew, K. L. "Family-School Relationship
Patterns: An Ecological Assessment." *School Psychology Review,* 1987, *16*(4), 498–512.

Quirk, J. P., and others. "Is Family Therapy Compatible with the
Public Schools, or Should They Be Divorced?" Paper Presented
at the Nineteenth Annual Convention of the National Association of School Psychologists, New Orleans, March 1987.

Rhodes, W. C. *The Emotionally Disturbed Student and Guidance.*
Boston: Houghton Mifflin, 1970.

Ribadeneira, D. "State Seeks Changes in Special Education." *Boston Globe,* Aug. 27, 1991.

Ron, K., Rosenberg, R., Melnick, T., and Pesses, D. "Family Therapy Alone Is Not Enough; or, The Dirty Story of Dorian." *Contemporary Family Therapy,* 1990, *12,* 35–48.

Rosenthal, R. *Experimental Effects in Behavioral Research.* New
York: Appleton-Century-Crofts, 1966.

Russell, M. L. "Behavioral Consultation: Theory and Process." *Personnel and Guidance Journal,* 1978, *56,* 346–350.

Santa Barbara, J., and others. "The McMaster Family Therapy Outcome Study: An Overview of Methods and Results." *International Journal of Family Therapy,* 1979, *1,* 304–323.

Shah, S. A. "Training and Utilizing a Mother as the Therapist for
Her Child." In B. G. Guerney (ed.), *Psychotherapeutic Agents:*

New Roles for Nonprofessionals. New York: Holt, Rinehart & Winston, 1969.

Smith, A. H. "Encountering the Family System in School Related Behavior Problems." *Psychology in the Schools,* 1978, *15,* 379–386.

Staver, N. "The Child's Learning Difficulty as Related to the Emotional Problems of the Mother." *American Journal of Orthopsychiatry,* 1953, *23,* 131–140.

Stone, G., and Peeks, B. "The Use of Strategic Family Therapy in the School Setting: A Case Study." *Journal of Counseling and Development,* 1986, *65*(12), 200–204.

Szapocznik, J., and others. "Conjoint Versus One-Person Family Therapy: Further Evidence for the Effectiveness of Conducting Family Therapy Through One Person with Drug-Abusing Adolescents." *Journal of Consulting and Clinical Psychology,* 1986, *54,* 395–397.

Szasz, T. *The Myth of Mental Illness.* New York: Harper & Row, 1961.

Tavormina, J. B. "Basic Models of Parent Counseling: A Critical Review." *Psychological Bulletin,* 1974, *81,* 827–835.

Taylor, D. "Family Consultation in a School Setting." *Journal of Adolescence,* 1982, *5*(4), 367–377.

Taylor, D. "The Child as Go-Between: Consulting with Parents and Teachers." *Journal of Family Therapy,* 1986, *8*(1), 79–89.

Tharp, R., and Wetzel, R. *Behavior Modification in the Natural Environment.* New York: Academic Press, 1969.

Tittler, B. I., and Cook, V. J. "Relationships Among Family, School, and Clinic: Toward a Systems Approach." *Journal of Clinical Child Psychology,* 1981, *10,* 184–187.

Tucker, B., and Dyson, E. "The Family and the School: Utilizing Human Resources to Promote Learning." *Family Process,* 1976, *15,* 125–142.

Ullmann, L. P., and Krasner, L. (eds.). *Case Studies in Behavior Modification.* New York: Holt, Rinehart & Winston, 1965.

von Bertalanffy, L. *General Systems Theory: Foundations, Developments, Applications.* New York: Braziller, 1968.

Wahler, R. G., Winkel, G. H., Peterson, R. F., and Morrison, D. C. "Mothers as Behavior Therapists for Their Own Children." In

A. M. Graziano (ed.), *Behavior Therapy with Children*. Chicago: Aldine-Atherton, 1971.

Wattenberg, S. H., and Kagle, J. D. "School Social Work Referrals for Family Therapy." *Social Work in Education*, 1986, *8*(4), 231–242.

Watzlawick, P., Weakland, J., and Fisch, R. *Change: Principles of Problem Formation and Problem Resolution*. New York: Norton, 1974.

Wendt, R. "Interview with Maurizio Andolfi." *Australian-New Zealand Journal of Family Therapy*, 1987, *8*, 153–157.

Wendt, R. "The Use of Systemic Provocation in Family Therapy for School Problems." In M. J. Fine and C. Carlson (eds.), *Handbook of Family-School Intervention: A Systems Perspective*. Boston: Allyn & Bacon, 1992.

Whitaker, C. "Psychotherapy of the Absurd with a Special Emphasis on the Psychotherapy of Aggression." *Family Process*, 1975, *14*, 1–16.

Willems, E. P. "Behavioral Technology and Behavioral Ecology." *Journal of Applied Behavioral Analysis*, 1974, *7*, 151–165.

Willems, E. P., and Stuart, D. G. "Behavioral Ecology as a Perspective on Marriages and Families." In J. P. Vincent (ed.), *Advances in Family Intervention, Assessment, and Theory*, Vol. I. Greenwich, Conn.: JAI Press, 1980.

Wolfendale, S. "Involving Parents in Behavior Management: A Whole School Approach." *Support for Learning*, 1986, *1*(4), 32–38.

Woody, R. H., Yeager, M., and Woody, J. D. "Appropriate Education for Handicapped Children: Introducing Family Therapy to School-Based Decision Making." *American Journal of Family Therapy*, 1990, *18*, 189–196.

Worden, M. "Classroom Behavior as a Function of the Family System." *School Counselor*, 1981, *28*, 178–188.

Wright, H. F. *Children's Behavior in Communities Differing in Size*. Lawrence: University of Kansas, 1970.

Wynne, L. C., McDaniel, S. H., and Weber, T. T. *Systems Consultation: A New Perspective for Family Therapy*. New York: Guilford Press, 1986.

Young, N. "Secondary School Counselors and Family Systems." *School Counselor,* 1979, *26,* 247–253.

Zins, J. E., and Hopkins, R. A. "Referral Out: Increasing the Number of Kept Appointments." *School Psychology Review,* 1981, *10,* 107–111.

Index

A

Accountability, obstacle of lack in, 156

Achievement, and intrapsychic misdiagnosis, 111–114

Administration, school, as collaborators, 46–47

Adult management deficit disorder (AMDD), diagnosis of, 75, 103–117

Alexander, F., 4

Alexander, J. F., 5

Amatea, E. S., 5, 13, 15, 20

American Association for Marriage and Family Therapy, 177, 179

American Psychological Association, 177–178

Anderson, C., 12

Anderson, J. S., 88

Andolfi, M., 9, 20, 30, 59

Angelo, C., 30, 59

Anger: and disagreement by managers, 121–124; parenting without, 97

Aponte, H. J., 6, 12, 15, 20, 55, 58

Apter, S. J., 5, 12

Assessment and intervention: collaborative, 23–36; consultant strategy meeting for, 23–25, 35; directness in, 61–62; and disagreement by managers, 119–120, 121–123, 125, 127–128; ecosystemic, 11–13; in extended families, 142–143, 144–145, 146, 148–149; goal for, 22; in intrapsychic misdiagnoses, 105–106, 108–110, 112–113, 114–115; locus of, 15–16; principles of, 21; School Decision Chart in, 31–36; skills in, 54–55; stage of, 51–52; with underinvolved family, 131–133, 135, 137, 138–139. *See also* Assessment skills; Intervention skills

DATE DUE

APR 1 1 1995			
DEC 0 5 2001			